MARTHA MORGAN'S LITTLE WORLD

The Essential Companion to the Angel Mountain Saga

Brian John

Brian John

Greencroft Books

2006

First Impression 2006

Copyright © Brian S John

Published by Greencroft Books
Trefelin, Cilgwyn, Newport,
Pembrokeshire SA42 0QN
Tel 01239-820470. Fax 01239-821245
Email: greencroft4@mac.com
Web: www.books-wales.co.uk

ISBN 0 905559 85 1

Typeset by the author in Palatino 10 pt and designed on
Apple iMac computer using Pages 2.0.2

Printed and bound in Wales by
Gwasg Gomer, Llandysul
Ceredigion SA44 4JL

Contents

Preface

This book has been written in response to many requests from the readers of the five novels of the Angel Mountain Saga for more information. When I have been out and about giving talks about the books, and during the course of literary walks, I am frequently asked detailed questions about places, characters, symbols, and folk traditions. There are many more questions of a broader nature about the landscape and environment of the area, and about the social history background to the stories. Some of the questions come from people who know the area around Carningli and Cilgwyn well, and others come from readers who have never even been to Pembrokeshire and who have their own mental picture of what Martha Morgan's Little World may have looked like.

So here it is -- a companion or guide to the series, which will, I hope, contain most of the things that anybody might wish to know. I have had to restrain myself on topics such as folklore, traditions and "great issues of the day" since this might otherwise have turned into an intimidating textbook rather than a comfortable companion! In assembling information I have been mindful of the wishes of some readers to delve more deeply; so I have provided them with information on my sources. I have also put in summaries of each of the stories, a full character list and a list of all Martha's diary entries.

But I have also been mindful of the requests from many readers for a beautifully illustrated book which will give them a "feel" for the area. That is difficult to do in an A5 format, which is of course needed if this book is to sit neatly in a bookshelf alongside the five novels. Many of the photographs are reproduced at a smaller scale than I would have liked, but I hope they will at least help to provide an attractive portrait of the locality.

This is not a book designed for reading from cover to cover. It is intended to be dipped into by readers who wish to obtain background material which might help them to understand the stories better -- not to mention Mistress Martha and the author!

For my wife
Inger
who is the inspiration for everything

1. The Saga

Set in West Wales in the late 1700's and early 1800's, the five novels record the life and times of Martha Morgan, the feisty and passionate Mistress of the small estate of Plas Ingli, on the flanks of Carningli (Angel Mountain) near Newport (Pembs). All five of the novels are best-sellers, and the saga has attracted a cult following. Partly, this interest arises from the personality of the heroine herself, who is described by reviewers as "fascinating, feisty, flawed, complex and tragic." She is a multi-faceted character, and as the Saga develops she shows herself to be passionate, compassionate, brave, impetuous, fiercely loyal and protective of family and servants, while at the same time suffering from bouts of insecurity and deep depression. Each novel brings out different aspects of her character and traces her growth as a person. She has supernatural powers, and feels in an almost mystical way that she is rooted in to the landscape and that the sacred mountain of Carningli is a part of her soul. She epitomises what is meant by the word *hiraeth*, and ultimately she may be seen as a symbol for Wales itself.

A manipulated photographic image, showing Plas Ingli where I want it to be!

The Saga

Then there are the other characters -- a host of very nasty villains, many who are partly good and occasionally bad, and the "angels" who help Martha to survive in the face of all the disasters that cruel fate decrees for her.

Joseph Harries the Wizard is a firm favourite with readers. Martha's daughter Daisy, the black sheep of the family, knows more than enough about the goings-on in Westminster to make a fallen angel blush. Then we have tough housekeeper Blodwen Owen, sage

The setting for the stories. The map is reasonably accurate, but it does contain some artistic license..........

and mentor Grandpa Isaac, the poetic and gentle Owain Laugharne, handmaiden Bessie Walter, smuggler Skiff Abraham, Patty the ex-prostitute, Brynach the foundling, political assassin Daniel O'Connell, rough industrialist Wilmot Gwynne, the preacher called Jones Minor Prophet, *Times* reporter Tom Foster, and many, many others..........

Publishing History

This is the full publishing history (to date) for the five novels:

On Angel Mountain by Brian John, Greencroft Books 2001. ISBN 0905559 80 0. A5 paperback, 328 pp. Published 30th September 2001. Reprinted 2003 and 2004. Total copies sold: 6,100

House of Angels by Brian John, Greencroft Books 2002. ISBN 0905559 81 9. A5 paperback, 432 pp, £7.99. Published 1st November 2002. Reprinted 2004. Total copies sold: 5,800

Dark Angel by Brian John, Greencroft Books 2003. ISBN 0905559 82 7. A5 paperback, 432 pp, £8.50. Published 1st November 2003. Reprinted 2005. Total copies sold: 4,800

Rebecca and the Angels by Brian John, Greencroft Books 2004. ISBN 0905559 83 5. A5 paperback, 432 pp. Published 1st November 2004. Reprinted 2006. Total copies sold: 3,300

Flying with Angels by Brian John, Greencroft Books, 2005, ISBN 0 905559 84 3. A5 paperback, 400 pp, £7.99. Published 30th October 2005. Total copies sold: 2,800

On Angel Mountain by Brian John, Corgi Books 2006. ISBN 9780552153270. Trade paperback, 462 pp, £6.99. Published 1st March 2006.

On Angel Mountain by Brian John, Clipper Audio 2006. Unabridged audiobook, ref H1957. ISBN: 1 84632 326 6. 11 cassettes, 15 hrs 15 mins. Price £45.95. Published June 2006.

House of Angels by Brian John, Corgi Books 2006. ISBN 9780552153287. Trade paperback, 554 pp, £6.99. Published 1st September 2006.

The Stories

In **On Angel Mountain** (Part One) eighteen-year-old Martha Morgan arrives at Plas Ingli, a small and vulnerable estate on the flank of Carningli (Angel Mountain) in North Pembrokeshire. The year is

The Saga

1796. She is pregnant and suicidal, having just been forced by her family into a hasty wedding. She is saved from harming herself or her unborn child by Joseph Harries the Wizard, who later becomes

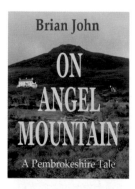

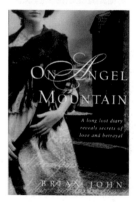

her mentor and friend. Joseph realizes that Martha has special powers, and she is very frightened when she experiences a number of visions and premonitions. She loves her husband David, and as she settles into the Plas she also learns to love the house and its extended family. But then she loses her baby and suffers from deep depression, and her resolve is further tested when there is a short-lived invasion by the French in 1797. Martha is increasingly concerned by the activities of a strange and sinister manservant called Moses Lloyd, and she becomes convinced that he is intent upon the destruction of the estate. After a number of misdemeanours he is sent packing, but Martha knows that he is not far away. Three local squires become increasingly antagonistic towards her and the estate, and matters come to a head when one of them, Alban Watkins, claims that the estate is rightfully his. David and his grandfather Isaac have to rush off to London to fight this claim in court. While they are away, Martha, who is pregnant again, has to face a trumped-up charge of theft. She is found guilty, and whipped through the streets of Newport. Then she is incarcerated in Haverfordwest Gaol. At last she manages to obtain her release through the good offices of Lord Cawdor. She returns home and receives a message to the effect that the court case is won, and that the estate is safe. Two of the villains are sentenced to transportation, and the other commits suicide. Martha needs space and peace in order to recover from her ordeal. She goes up to her secret cave on the mountain, and is captured there by Moses Lloyd, who knew that she would eventually come. He is intent upon raping Martha and then killing her, but in a frantic struggle she kills him. She disposes of his body in a deep crevice and crawls home, more dead than alive.

In *House of Angels* (Part Two) Martha learns much about the brutality of the world, and about the devastating effect that her beauty has on the men with whom she comes in contact. She also learns a good deal about her own strength in the face of adversity. In the year 1805, her husband David is killed in the annual *cnapan* contest on Newport Sands, leaving her with three young children to bring up alone. She is also pregnant. She is helped through the crisis by her servants and friends, and her fourth child is born. Joseph is convinced that David's death was not an accident, and his investigations lead him to the conclusion that four men -- Matthew Lloyd, Joseph Rice, John Howell and Ifan Beynon -- are guilty of murder. The four villains, together with two strange Londoners and a squire's son named John Fenton, are intent upon the destruction of the estate because they are convinced that there is treasure hidden on Plas Ingli land. Indeed there is, but only Martha knows where it is. As the story proceeds, Martha falls in love with Owain, the younger son of a local squire, and their love affair is anything but smooth. Alban Watkins, the dastardly squire who claimed the estate in 1797, suddenly returns from the colonies, also intent upon finding the Plas Ingli treasure. Martha orchestrates a treasure hunt, which results in the capture of all of the villains. In the court cases that follow, David's murderers are all sentenced to hang, and the other treasure

Brian John

hunters to transportation. But two of the villains manage to escape. One of them, Alban Watkins, is murdered by an Irishman in revenge for atrocities committed in the penal colonies. The other, John Fenton, abducts little Sara, and entices Martha to a lonely cottage where she hopes to obtain her daughter's release. Fenton has always lusted after Martha, and he attempts to rape her; but Owain intervenes in the nick of time, and following a ferocious struggle Fenton escapes, only to be sucked to his death in a nearby bog.

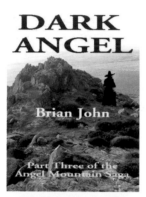

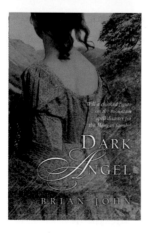

In *Dark Angel* (Part Three) the story starts in 1807 with Martha and Owain deeply in love, and engaged to be married. Martha has premonitions of dark and tragic events to come, and her unease is increased by sightings of a mysterious figure in black on the mountain. He appears to be watching her, and when others see the figure as well he is given the name of "The Nightwalker." Martha is uncertain whether he is a man, or a ghost, or the Devil himself. She becomes quite paranoid, but her attention is diverted when a small baby is left on the front doorstep of the Plas. Martha names the child Brynach, and arranges to adopt him. Plans are made for the wedding, but then Owain goes out on a fishing trip and disappears without trace. Joseph investigates, and deduces that a squire called George Price has arranged for the sabotage of Owain's boat. Again Martha becomes depressed and paranoid, and very possessive about the baby. She gets some straight talking from her nearest and dearest. Over the years that follow the Nightwalker appears over and again, and Martha suspects that Joseph Har-

The Saga

ries the wizard, and even her servants, know more about the creature than she does. She has to face further tragedy: her daughter Daisy goes off to London and breaks off all contact with the family, and her son Dewi is drowned at sea. In 1822, under pressure from family and friends, Martha agrees to marry again. Squire Ceredig ap Tomos proposes, and she accepts. On the night of the wedding Owain returns from the dead, and Martha has no option but to choose him over Ceredig. She is horrified when the man she has rejected commits suicide. Owain is also ill, having experienced appalling hardship in North Africa and Spain, and she tries to nurse him back to good health. Exhausted by all this emotional turmoil, Martha goes to her cave for silence and contemplation, but comes face to face with the Nightwalker. He is terribly disfigured and injured as a result of an accident in the Napoleonic Wars, and he proves to be Iestyn Price, the son of Squire Price and the father of the child left on the doorstep of the Plas fifteen years earlier. Iestyn tells Martha that Brynach's mother is none other than Elen, her sister who emigrated to America shortly after the birth. He is reconciled with his father, but he dies within a few days of his encounter with Martha, and is buried secretly in his father's walled garden.

In *Rebecca and the Angels* (Part Four) Martha is a mature and confident woman in charge of her own destiny. Brynach is married, and has inherited the Llanychaer estate. The story covers the years 1832-1844. Martha recounts the loss of Owain and Joseph, and finally the death of her daughter Sara. She becomes increasingly aware of political issues, and decides to fight for social justice in order to make her mark on history. She is dragged into the controversy involving the corrupt turnpike trusts in West Wales, and at first tries to mediate between the labourers and the squires in order to minimise the suffering associated with unjust tollgate charges.

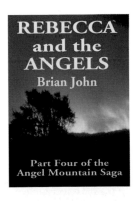

The Saga

But she gets nowhere. Hardship increases, and the Rebecca Riots commence. Men with blackened faces and dressed in female garb ride out and smash down tollgates all over West Wales. Martha becomes more and more involved behind the scenes, and eventually finds a role as one of those orchestrating events. As the turnpike trusts and the authorities seek to enforce law and order, the Army is called in, and Martha starts to cooperate with solicitor Hugh Williams in her attempts to keep one step ahead. She also develops an unlikely friendship with Tom Foster, a reporter from the *Times* newspaper. Spies begin to operate in the area, and some of the rioters are arrested as a result of information provided by a traitor. He is identified and hunted down. Martha is suspected by the authorities of involvement in the riots, and a complex game of cat and mouse develops. With matters building towards a climax, Martha makes a foolhardy gesture and takes part in a raid on the Boncath tollgate. She is lucky to escape relatively unscathed, and thinks that it is time to retire from any further involvement with the rioters. But in a final terrifying twist to the story a gang of criminals moves into the area and Martha has to confront its leaders in the kitchen of the Plas. She saves her female servants from rape and kills two of the thugs. She fears that she will be charged with murder, but is deemed by the magistrates to have acted in self-defence. Finally, her long-lost daughter Daisy returns from London, and with her assistance a new Act of Parliament is passed which addresses all of the abuses associated with the turnpike trusts.

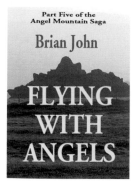

Part Five of the
Angel Mountain Saga

Brian John

FLYING
WITH
ANGELS

In *Flying with Angels* (Part Five) Martha grows old disgracefully and reaches the end of her eventful journey through life. This is a complex and tragic tale in which our heroine confronts the realities of growing old, and in which personal crises are juxtaposed with great events on the world stage. It is 1845, and Martha is feeling her age. But as she dreams of a peaceful dotage, she receives

The Saga

The Cwm -- the amphitheatre in which most of the action of the stories occurs

warnings that she should "take care". Her beloved estate collapses, and she has to call upon her deepest reserves of strength in order to survive. But her misery is lessened when the new owner of the Plas Ingli estate turns out to be one Wilmot Gwynne, a self-made man who is as generous as he is eccentric. Brynach blames himself for the collapse of the estate, and when Martha tells him everything about his parentage he decides to emigrate to America, taking his son David with him. Martha knows that she will never see them again. She meets a travelling evangelist on the summit of Angel Mountain. It turns out that the fate of Amos Jones Minor Prophet is inextricably bound up with her own. They grow closer, and a single indiscretion in Tycanol Wood splits the community and tests the loyalty of friends and family to the limit. This starts a drift towards the final

The Saga

tragic episodes of Martha's life. While she is dealing with personal crises, she is also drawn to help the peasants caught up in the Irish Potato Famine of 1845-48. A shipwreck on the coast near Newport gives her the opportunity to do something practical, but in the process she offends the secret Society of Sea Serjeants. Her family tries to protect her from evil men who are driven by ancient family animosities. But her fighting spirit is stronger than her body, and she takes them on. It becomes clear that Martha will not die in her bed; nor does she, but in the final act of her life there are breathless twists and turns which confound her enemies. Amos sacrifices himself for her, and she dies on her beloved mountain, unbowed and undefeated.

Sunset and calm sea, Newport Bay. Dinas Head is on the left

Themes

The Saga as a whole is about resilience, love and honour, and about the ability of the human spirit to conquer brutality, betrayal and all manner of other evils. Mistress Martha is no paragon of virtue, but I hope that she is close enough to "everyman" and "everywoman" to give comfort and inspiration to at least some of my readers.

Part One is about a naive and frightened young woman who learns -- the hard way -- how to survive when she is confronted by monstrous wickedness.

Part Two (the most complex of the five novels) is about Martha's recognition of her own strength and about taking responsibility for the righting of wrongs; it is also about the dangers of vengeance, arrogance and manipulation.

Part Three (a much darker and more introverted novel) is about loss, insecurity, mistrust and paranoia.

Part Four is about Martha in middle age, deciding to use her talents to try and make the world a better place.

And Part Five is about the dilemmas of old age, with Martha trying to live life to the full, and give her love to others, while confronting the inevitability of death.

Although many deaths and many shocking and brutal incidents are described in the pages of the novels, there are also many

counterbalancing episodes of love and laughter, serenity and beauty. I see the five books as ultimately optimistic, and about the triumph of good over evil.

The Reviews

There are very many reviews of the books in newspapers, in journals and on the web. Here is a small selection:

For *On Angel Mountain*

A fast-paced plot ..... overall, this is a novel that is difficult to put down. *Mehanz Young, New Books Magazine*

Unusual and beautifully written...there are shades of Thomas Hardy's Wessex. *Nottingham Evening Post*

If it does not become a best-seller, there is no justice in this world. *John Seymour, writer and broadcaster*

A modern Welsh literary triumph... An excellent evocation of the beautiful countryside of the area and the traditions of rural eighteenth-century Wales. It has a page-turning plot, packed with adventure, treason, murder and passion, where the horrors in the drama are balanced by gentle scenes full of the warmth and love of the family at Plas Ingli. And it has, in Martha Morgan, an irresistible narrator and heroine: brave, impetuous, loving, and occasionally vengeful....... *Welsh Books Council*

The writing is vibrant and alive. For someone who had never written fiction before some of the erotic scenes -- not to mention a brilliantly crafted description of a miscarriage -- needed careful handling........ The author lives in one of the most beautiful parts of Britain, and he has used that landscape and scenery to fuel his imagination. *Phil Carradice, Writers' Forum*

Need a book to snuggle up with by the fire? This is it -- a stirring tale of the rebuilding of the fortunes of a Pembrokeshire farming

The Saga

Flaming Maytime gorse on the mountain

family told through the diary of the young mistress of the house. It's got the lot -- love, nature, mystery, mysticism and a lot of charm -- a bit Wilkie Collins. The period detail is so authentic you forget it's recently written, and it's one of those books you miss when you've finished it. *Welsh Living*

The concept is imaginative and enjoyable. The book will unquestionably enjoy an audience not only in Wales, but for anyone with the remotest interest in our nation. *Western Mail*

It is a sign of the writer's skill and imagination that we enter fully into Martha's vivid world. If you want to enjoy a lively, skillful and exciting portrayal of real life in eighteenth-century Pembrokeshire, you will have to buy this book. *County Echo*

The author's intimate knowledge of the subject is apparent on every page. The story is soundly based on historical fact, and allusions to genuine historical people and events give it a feeling of

The Saga

authenticity. But this is more than just a diary of a country lady. Cleverly woven into the text runs a dark and sinister tale.... This book will give pleasure to those who are fascinated by social history and to those who enjoy a gripping tale. *Gwales (Welsh Books Council)*

A well-paced and well-plotted tale with a gripping finale and a strong sense of place. *Pembrokeshire Life*

For *House of Angels*

Comments from pre-publication reviews by referees:

"Placed in the setting of Angel Mountain and the surrounding countryside, this is an exciting story of intrigue, with villains galore, but given a feminine twist by the heroine Martha and her friends, family and servants.

The diary format is cleverly used to push the story along -- at the end of each chapter, the reader just has to press on to the next. But one is led carefully through the complex story without ever getting lost."

"The book portrays the heroine's complex and changeable temperament and shows how she copes with life in a harsh and cruel world. It shows her humour, her strengths and her weaknesses, and because she is far from perfect one likes her all the more.

I loved the accelerating pace towards the end of the book, and especially the climax itself."

"There is a tangible reality about Martha. From the honesty of her diary entries she emerges as no perfect lady but as a flawed heroine. She drags you down with her in her battles against depression and carries you up with her into the bliss of new love and the joys of motherhood."

The Saga

Published Reviews

Martha Morgan becomes a very real person and the books are a compulsive read, with shades of Cordell and Cookson, although the author refutes outside influences apart from the brooding presence of Carningli itself. *Derek Rees, Western Telegraph*

Readers are swept along on a roller-coaster of emotion, experiencing Martha's passionate love for her family and their mountainside home to her desire for truth and justice. The plot twists and turns with murder, hidden treasure and romance all preventing the

Late evening amid the crags on the summit of Carningli

reader from putting the book down until finished. I look forward to further offerings from Brian John and his inspiring heroine Martha Morgan." *Catherine Collins, County Echo*

This is a splendidly-imagined and well-told tale of good triumphing over evil, set in the dramatic scenery of Carningli near Newport, Pembrokeshire. ...the local colour is brilliantly imagined and the incidental historical detail, unobtrusively woven into the fabric of the narrative, is fascinating. Here is an adventure story in

Old ash trees on the wall adjacent to Carningli Lodge

which the narrative never flags. The delineation of the main characters, especially the headstrong and irresistible Mistress Martha, by turns spiritual and earthy, is vivid and true. *Robert Anthony, Western Telegraph*

   This time the beauty (Martha Morgan) is swept through a complex tale of murder, intrigue and romance. Mixing grief and pathos, exuberance and humour in equal measure, the whole narrative has a strong sense of place. *Dean Powell, Western Mail*

   The beauty of the country and the day to day business of farm life is set amidst intrigue and a collection of compelling characters to make a wonderful winter read. *Welsh Living*

The Saga

Martha Morgan, who is young and beautiful, tells the story through entries in her journal, with many descriptions of local characters and customs and so lyrical a response to the beauty of the landscape that she might have been influenced by Dorothy Wordsworth..... All this is satisfying and well told...... In terms of presentation other publishers might learn a few tricks. *Richard Jones, Planet*

Based on her diary, this novel, like its predecessor, reaches out and pulls you into Martha's small world..... Beautifully written, this book takes you on a journey which you will never forget. If it is not made into a lavish period drama for the television there is no justice! *Jo Barnes, One Wales magazine*

For *Dark Angel*

Comments from Readers:

"Like many readers, I'm already caught up in the dramatic events of the saga and in the heroine's emotional complexity."
"Beautifully written from cover to cover"
"Once again, you have shown that you know just how to spin a good yarn."
"........ the story just gets better and better!"
"........ a series run through with the raw energy of the North Pembrokeshire environment."
"...... as exciting and interesting as ever. How long must we wait for the next story in the series?"
"A colourful tale full of tension and with authentic period detail."
"......... enchanting and mysterious..."
"A tale of a complex, compelling creature on a voyage of discovery."

The Saga

Published Reviews

An excellent book which recounts the further adventures of Mistress Martha Morgan of Plas Ingli -- who is now firmly established as one of the most interesting heroines in recent historical fiction. Move over, Elizabeth Bennett! Really this tale, set in the early 1800's, is all

Cliff face on Carningli

about love lost and regained, and while the story is dominated by a mysterious figure in black called "The Nightwalker", and by the heroine's self-doubts and periods of depression, this novel is really about constancy and the triumph of love. As in the earlier novels, the plot twists and turns and rushes ahead at a fine pace, and once again the author packs a double whammy into the final few pages of the book. *Amazon.com*

The author has woven timelessness into the character of Martha Morgan. This is a love story, a tale of a complex, compelling creature on a voyage of discovery that veers between elation and despair and of a love lost and found. Martha reveals through her diary entries every innermost secret of her being. It reveals a driving force she at times cannot control. Martha has an eye for the most intimate detail of people and things; she is complex and mysterious, at times ruthless, yet it would appear she is insecure, in spite of the warmth and advice of the people who surround her. Whatever worms of discontent writhe in Martha's breast, be it passion, self-analysis or the nightmare of the Nightwalker, she is revealed as a creature of innate strength. This book is filled with goodness; it is filled with caring, compassionate people. It has a message that basically the human species recognizes truth, justice, fairness and kindness. Martha dominates this book. Her mysticism, and meditations on the mountain, her joys and sadness perhaps reveal the fragility seldom perceived in the Martha Morgans of this present day world. It is a timeless and compelling tale. *Richard Cluroe, Gwales.com*

What a synopsis doesn't mention is the richly textured background against which the drama is all played out; the deep, underlying sense of place; the wisdom and humour of ordinary (and sometimes extraordinary) folk; and the keenly researched and observed cameos of rural life in the community, living and working in the protective shadow of Angel Mountain. *Irene Payne, Western Telegraph*

For *Rebecca and the Angels*

Comments from Readers:

"By quite a long way the best of the Angel Mountain series....... the author skillfully conjures a part for Martha in the planning and execution of the protests against the hated toll-gates, and constructs from this involvement a powerful and at times horrific piece of fiction. A first-class read!" *Fred Nicholls*

"For me, the best yet. The exploits of the real and imaginary characters are woven together wonderfully well, and the dialogue is convincing. A very easy and satisfying read. As with the previous volumes, the pace cannot be faulted. Suspense and interest is maintained throughout......." *Robert Anthony*

"I think this is the best yet. The story rips along at a fine pace, with many twists and turns. Very moving at times, and occasionally brutal. Overall, the book is enjoyable, credible and well written." *Ian Richardson*

Published Reviews:

The unique perspective which the author brings to his robust saga of Pembrokeshire country folk ..... manages to make even the most familiar aspects of the Rebecca tale seem fresh, and arguably this is the most successful of the series to date. Once again the action builds to a dramatic denouement on the slopes of Carningli, and in the final

Old gatepost at Carningli Lodge

showdown the spirited Martha once again confounds all those foolish enough to think of conspiring against her and her flock of guardian angels. *Keith Johnson, Pembrokeshire Life*

The magic of Martha Morgan and the mystical mountain of Carningli continues to weave its spell. In "Rebecca and the Angels" author Brian John's storytelling reaches a rich maturity. We are

The Saga

swept along in a gripping tale that often leaves you breathless. I'm delighted that Brian's books have been snapped up by Transworld Publishers and that readers throughhout the world will now be able to share in Martha's magic." *Doris Goddard, Western Telegraph*

The author has researched his period well and is at ease with his genre. The pace is, like the Welsh climate, gentle one minute, tempestuous the next, ranging from blood, battles, intrigue and treachery to the whimsical, fly, romantic and mystical. The author's obvious appreciation of the Welsh countryside comes across to the reader in some excellent descriptive prose; indeed, like its heroine, this is a book of many parts. *Norma Penfold, Gwales.com (Welsh Books Council)*

For *Flying with Angels*

Published Reviews:

This novel has all the feisty and awe-inspiring ingredients to be found in John's preceding books relating to Martha - and many of the original characters remain as alive and colourful as ever, together with several new and animated individuals who add still more flavour to the narrative. As always Martha finds a cause to fight for, and this time it is the Poor Irish, caught up in the Potato Famine of 1845-48. She becomes embroiled in a private battle with the secret Society of Sea Serjeants, and this gives her friends and family some considerable problems as they try to protect her from the society's vengeance. John, as always, has a magical feeling of place and his narrative is full of dynamism and perception.
Norma Penfold, Gwales.com (Welsh Books Council)

The much loved Angel Mountain books take the form of a discovered diary, which follows the life of insuppressible heroine Mistress Martha Morgan from her late teenage years to her demise in this the final book.........Wackier she may get but it is apparent that Mistress Martha has lost none of the saltiness and spirit that have endeared her to readers since the first book called "On Angel Mountain" appeared from the author's own publishing imprint, Greencroft Books. *Becky Hotchin, PembrokeshireTV*

Successive books have turned Martha into Pembrokeshire's best-loved fictional character. The books have also turned Carningli (the key location in the saga, and the place where Martha has her secret cave) into a place of pilgrimage, climbed by many readers who generally stay well clear of mountains. Brian blames the "spirit of the mountain" for that phenomenon, but the books clearly have something to do with it.
News Wales (Western Mail)

The old track onto the common from Carningli Lodge

The Saga

Readers' Comments

"Another masterpiece -- real, full of passion and substance,
 guts, love, life and death -- and more -- in all their beauty."
"A magnificent achievement. Well up to the standard of
previous books; pacy, racy and full of dramatic and romantic
incident."
"The Introduction is original, touching and full of humanity.
Thoroughly believable."
"The book has a very interesting story line, and as ever the
 narrative moves along at a cracking pace."
"Quite an episode -- a real tear-jerker........"
"Well done! A lot of loose ends are very neatly tied up."
"This book features some delightful and refreshing new
characters."
"It's good to see that in spite of everything Martha has not lost
her sense of humour -- the book is full of striking images and
witty one-liners."
"Martha is as feisty and sensuous as ever, and grows ever
more eccentric."
"I really love the way you handle the winding-down at the
end of the book. The final pages could have been sentimental,
but I found the writing sparse, economical and very effective.
I wept."

On getting into print

Novelists invariably think that their works are superior to anything
else in print, and that they deserve to be international best-sellers.
They cannot understand the success of inferior novels like *Pride and
Prejudice* and *The Da Vinci Code*, and neither can they understand it
when others (including agents and publishers) fail to appreciate their
talents! But they remain optimistic, even though they know that
only a small percentage of written novels actually become published

The Saga

novels. So they send off their first chapters, with polite letters and covering materials designed to tempt and even excite those who sit in judgement, knowing that at one end of the scale of publishing success is the million pound advance, and at the other end is the slush pile.

So it was when I had finished writing *On Angel Mountain* in 2001. The writing process had taken me about 18 months. The manuscript had been read by family and friends, and they had all said "This is great! It must be published!" Thus encouraged, and with warm support from the Welsh Books Council and from established Welsh authors like Iris Gower and Catrin Collier, I started on the process of contacting prospective publishers. I did not try the Welsh publishers, since I knew that in Wales I could sell as many copies as they could if I was forced, in the end, to publish myself. So I went for the mainstream London publishers -- more than 50 of them by the time I gave up on the idea. Only one or two actually read my sample chapter. The great majority did not reply. Some returned my material unopened and unread, with standard replies attached: "We are very sorry, but our publishing lists are full. We are not taking on any new authors just now. Our fiction programme is being cut back. There is no market for historical fiction set in Wales. And by the way, we do not deal with authors direct. Please go away and find an agent."

I was of course discouraged, but determined to keep trying. So I contacted 54 carefully selected agents by telephone and letter and got standard replies from them too: "We are very sorry, but we are not taking on any new authors just now. If you like, we will read and assess your material in exchange for a large fee. And by the way, there is no market for historical fiction set in Wales."

There was no alternative, if I wanted my story to see the light of day, but to go it alone. Then I remembered the old adage: beware of vanity, and beware even more of vanity publishing. I had visions of bedrooms and attics full of unopened boxes of books and realised that if people did not like *On Angel Mountain* that would be its fate. I needed more advice. So I printed off five full copies of the manu-

The Saga

Carningli Lodge and its bounding walls, seen from the mountain

script and sent it to friends whom I could trust to give me their opinions honestly, and to advise me -- if necessary -- to forget about the idea of being a novelist. They all came back to me within a few weeks and said "Very enjoyable! Go for it!" So I did.

The business of publishing was perfectly familiar, and I had no problem with it. It simply involved a lot of hard work, with long hours in front of the computer. The text had to be edited and finalised. Then it had to be reformatted and paginated, with decisions made on typeface, type size, style of headings and so forth. I decided to go for a full A5 format, somewhat bigger than trade paperback size, because I wanted the book to be big and brash and to sell the message: "This is a novel set in Pembrokeshire. If you love the county, you must buy it!" I could not afford to hire a specialist designer, so I made the cover myself, using my own photography and an old Adobe programme called PhotoDeluxe -- a poor man's version of Photoshop. Then, having worked out the book dimensions and number of pages, I obtained printing quotes. I would have liked to print the book in Wales, but discovered that none of the Welsh printers stocked the right sort of bulky "mass market" paper required and that their prices were more than double those of the specialist paperback printers in England. So the book was printed eventually by CPI Bath Press. They did an excellent job.

The book was launched on 30th September 2001 at a jolly event in the Newport Boat Club. We had readings, wine and nibbles, and there was tremendous support from friends, family, and people from far and wide who had bought non-fiction books of mine in the past. In a welter of press releases, reviews, photographs and interviews, Mistress Martha was introduced to the world.

It soon became apparent that readers liked the books and loved Mistress Martha! The early reviews of the book were also very encouraging. With sales rising steadily and with frequent requests for a sequel, I thought for a while and then decided to get stuck in -- there would be four additional novels covering other key phases in

The author on the mountain, with the Parrog and Newport Bay in the distance

Martha's life, to be written and published within four years. That was a very ambitious target, and I was not sure that I could work so quickly -- but in the spring of 2002 I decided on rough synopses for the four future books, breaking up into manageable slices the rest of Martha's story that was still in my head. I started work on *House of Angels* in April 2002 and fin-

The Saga

ished the writing at the beginning of August. The next three months were devoted to editing, refereeing, typesetting, book design, printing and publishing. As before, I used my "referees' panel" and obtained advice from its members on anachronisms, inconsistencies or unconvincing sections of text. At last I was happy, and the book appeared at the beginning of November. The winter of 2002-2003 was devoted to publicity and marketing, with some weeks of relaxation dotted about here and there. But there was not that much lazing about, for my mind was already mulling over the storyline for *Dark Angel* and my holiday reading was mostly to do with the history and social history of early nineteenth-century Wales.

After that I stuck to the same routine each year -- effectively four months of research and writing, four months devoted to the publishing process, and four months for marketing, publicity, recuperation and mental preparation for the next writing stint! So 2003 was the year of *Dark Angel*, 2004 the year of *Rebecca and the Angels*, and 2005 the year of *Flying with Angels*. I tried not to become a hermit while the writing was going on, and Inger and I still managed to get to Sweden each summer to visit all of our Swedish relatives, and we also managed trips to Australia, New Zealand, Brittany and Gran Canaria. In strange and unpredictable ways those trips fed into the stories; holiday reading gave me background material, and in two visits to "Ned Kelly Country" in the hinterland of Melbourne I was inspired by the mythology and the tragedy of the penal colonies to the extent that I had to build them into the Angel Mountain books. The only major interference with the writing process occurred in August 2004, when I poured burning wax all over my right foot, and various other bits of my anatomy, and ended up in the Burns Unit of Morriston Hospital. Luckily my two index fingers were not affected, and so I was able to keep on writing. That, in case anybody wondered, explains the dedication in the front of *Rebecca and the Angels*, and the rather lurid front cover!

At the end of August 2005 the writing was done, and Mistress Martha was in her grave. More than a million words banged into my computer using my trusty two-fingered technique. It was a time of mixed emotions. On the one hand there was a sadness that my time spent in the company of the beautiful and eccentric Mistress of Plas Ingli was at an end, and that there was now a void in my life that I would have to fill in other ways. But on the other hand there was relief that I had managed to write, publish and sell five big novels in five years while still retaining my sanity (but maybe that's for others to judge!) and without too many disruptions to family life. For that, Inger deserves huge credit, for she has been mentor, sounding-board, reader and proof-reader, and head consultant on the female psyche -- as well as being a loving wife, chasing me out of the house and up onto the mountain whenever she felt that I needed to get away from that glowing computer screen two feet in front of my nose.

And one adventure leads on and into another. For the immediate future, I need to work closely with Transworld Publishers, who have bought the English-language rights to the first three parts of the Saga. The company is part of the vast Random House group which publishes under many different imprints -- Corgi, Random House, Black Swan, Bantam, Ebury, Vintage and many others. Novelists published by the Group include Dan Brown, Jilly Cooper, Sebastian Foulks, John Grisham, Robert Harris, Ian McEwan and Terry Pratchett. Transworld is always on the lookout for new authors, and in 2004, while I was still at work on *Rebecca and the Angels*, I received a message out of the blue from Corgi editor Gail Haslam offering a contract for the publication of the first three volumes of the series. I had received clues that something was in the wind, since my old friend Marley Davies of Victoria Bookshop in Haverfordwest had told me that certain mainstream publishers had picked up on the success of the novels in Wales and had obtained copies for reading by their editorial teams. Gail now told me that she and her colleagues loved the books and wanted them for the Corgi list. By December 2004 the deal was done, and a publishing schedule for the three books was agreed. At the time of writing the Corgi editions of *On Angel Mountain* and *House of Angels* are already in print, with wonderful new covers and a slightly smaller format than the Green-

The Saga

croft books editions. I have not made a fortune out of them yet, but hope springs eternal.........

One final development is the issue of the unabridged audio version of *On Angel Mountain* in July 2006. Eleven tapes and more than fifteen hours of listening! The narrators are Jonathan Keeble and Leanne Masterton, and having listened to some of the tapes I must say that I'm very happy, especially with the way in which Leanne's voice fits the character of Mistress Martha. It's great that the book is now available to blind people and those who prefer to listen rather than read.

Maytime on the mountain, with the fresh green leaves of bilberry prominent on the lower scree slopes

Carningli on a bright May day, seen from the Clydach Valley, not far from Llwyngwair Lodge

2. The Origins of the Story

A Very Strange Episode

Over the course of the last forty years I have written more than 60 books, but I have never had any great urge to write fiction. My wife Inger has often encouraged me to "write a novel", but I have always refused on the grounds that the world of fiction is alien territory in which I would probably feel out of place and even hopelessly lost. Then something happened which was very strange indeed -- and almost spooky.............

In 1999 Inger and I travelled to Gran Canaria for a short holiday, and en route I picked up a strange virus on the aircraft. I felt ill even before we landed, but on arrival I experienced classic flu-like symptoms, including a high temperature, headache, heavy limbs, and episodes of shivering. I went straight to bed when we arrived at the apartment, and I spent the whole of the night wide awake, feeling horrible and sweating gallons. During this strange delirious episode, a story came into my head -- of a feisty and passionate woman called Martha Morgan. (At first I thought her name was Mary, but then I realized that only Martha would do.) As I lay there in the warm darkness, gazing at the bedroom ceiling, I tuned in to dates, places, characters, and a storyline covering the whole of Martha's exciting life between 1796 (when she was still a teenager) and the time of her death in 1855. Somehow or other, individual episodes came into my head, and I even picked up on key conversations in considerable detail. I knew that the story had to be told in the words of Mistress Martha, not retrospectively but with immediacy, through diary entries.

In the morning, not having slept a wink, I felt better, but the story was fixed firmly inside my head. (If the story had come to me in a dream, it would certainly have disappeared from my memory by breakfast time.) I told Inger about this strange experience, and she said "Well then, you'd better start writing!" So I did..

I still do not know what to make of that strange episode. At least, I now know what the term "fevered imagination" means! But I still think that in some strange way the story was "given" to me, and that I had to keep faith with this exotic and imperfect creature called Mistress Martha. For better or for worse, in spite of the fact that I was a 59-year-old grandfather, I had to try and put into words the emotions and the experiences of a pregnant, suicidal 18-year-old female who lived more than 200 years ago, and I had to do it in the most difficult of formats -- the daily diary. My family and friends probably thought I was nuts, but to their credit they did not try to discourage me!

Since the publication of *On Angel Mountain* in 2001 I have been asked on innumerable occasions whether there really was a woman called Martha Morgan who lived and died in North Pembrokeshire at the time of the saga. After all, they say, if the story came to me as a gift, who was the donor if not Martha herself, or her spirit? I am intrigued by ghosts and spirits, and certainly do not dismiss them out of hand -- and I have done my duty, in the interests of science, by searching through the old records for somebody called Martha Morgan who might have been the Mistress of a failing estate in the early years of the nineteenth century. I have found several Martha Morgans, but they all seem to have been lowly people who lived in places as far afield as St David's and St Dogmaels. I have found one Martha Morgan in the Newport area, but she lived much later than my heroine. So if there was a "real" Martha Morgan in or near Newport in the early 1800's, I have not found her yet.........

Another wonderful discovery for me (as a novice in the business) is the manner in which readers become totally involved with the characters, especially Mistress Martha, Bessie her faithful maid, and Joseph Harries the Wizard. Readers have told me that they sometimes get very angry with Martha, and that they laugh with her in her times of joy and cry with her when she struggles against misfortune. That, of course, is what an author wants to hear. Quite a few male readers have told me, as the saga has proceeded, that they are more than a little in love with Mistress Martha, and some female readers have admitted to a secret passion for Joseph. They have also told me, when I have fulfilled my sad duty of "killing off" their favourite characters, that they have grieved as if for the loss of a loved one.

Mixing Fact and Fiction

Now that there is something of a cult following for the novels, one of my greatest tasks is to disabuse people who believe that the diaries really did exist, and that the "real" Martha Morgan is not buried in

Epitaph to Thomas James, Squire of Gelli Fawr, who died in 1801 and was buried in the family enclosure in Cilgwyn Churchyard

Cilgwyn Churchyard. (The walled family enclosure in the churchyard actually contains the remains of the James family of Gelli Fawr.) But I am delighted that my method of mixing fact and fiction -- some real characters and some fictional ones, some real places and some imagined -- seems to have worked.

Authenticity is of course crucial in historical fiction, and a lot of serious research had to go into matters like the French Invasion, the decline of the gentry, seasonal traditions in the Pembrokeshire countryside, the Rebecca Riots, the Australian penal colonies, and the Irish Potato Famine. Then there were the broader issues that a liberal female like Martha would have followed avidly -- Chartism, smuggling activities, prison reform, the anti-slavery movement, the abuses which disfigured the Turnpike Trusts, the evils of the justice system, trade manipulation by merchants and secret societies, and the non-conformist religious revivals. All of these great issues make appearances in the stories, and some understanding of them is essential if the reader is to fully understand why Martha gets drawn into them even when she would have been wiser to have stayed at home playing her harp. There is more detail in Chapter 8, but a few comments at this stage are appropriate.

Sign on the front of the Royal Oak Inn, Fishguard

The French Invasion of 1797. This was the last occasion on which foreign troops marched on British soil with aggressive intent. Actually the intent was more aggressive than the reality. Since I was a child I have been fascinated by the tragi-comedy of the event and by some of the myths surrounding it -- such as the tale of the tough cobbler-woman called Jemima Nicholas. Since the invasion was of both local and national significance, it had to be incorporated into the first novel, giving me the opportunity to show Martha's steadfast resolve, David's courage, and Moses Lloyd's cowardice. I researched the sequence of events vary carefully, and I have taken virtually no liberties with the facts in the recounting of what happened. So in sense, the episode in *On Angel Mountain* is really history with a thin layer of fiction added on top to give it flavour.

The Rebecca Riots. These iconic episodes of discontent were also of immense importance in West Wales, and they played a key part in British history, as we shall see later, in Chapter 7. Again, I have been fascinated for many years by the mythology associated with the riots. The pictures which I have held in my head since childhood are wonderful -- the image of the huge prize-fighter Twm

An artist's impression of one of the Rebecca Riots -- but note that he has forgotten the blackened faces!

Carnabwth, black-faced and fitted out in the largest gown and shawl he could find, leading the first riot at Efailwen. The image of hordes of men dressed as women, leading the smartly-dressed and mounted troops of the Dragoons a merry dance across a dark and inhospitable countryside. Wonderful -- and quite irresistible. The fourth novel in the series, dealing with Martha's sympathy for the underclass and her involvement in the riots, is the most "political" of all the stories. I have tried to make the social and political context accurate, and many of the episodes recounted really did happen. Some of the key characters were indeed closely involved in the events of the day: for example solicitor Hugh Williams, Times reporter Thomas Campbell Foster, Colonel James Frederick Love, toll-farmer Thomas Bullin, and the villains Shoni Sgubor Fawr and Dai'r Cantwr. These last two really did introduce a criminal and thuggish component to the riots, but they did not (as far as I am aware) actually penetrate as far west as Newport (Pembs). And I have to admit to inventing one or two turnpike trusts and a few toll-gates for the purposes of the story! I put a disclaimer on page 428 of the book just in case anybody might be moved to look on it as a piece of history rather than fiction.

The Australian Dimension. Some readers are intrigued by the part which Australia plays in these novels of west Wales. At the end of the first book some of the villains are shipped off to the penal colonies, and in *House of Angels* one of them -- the devious and mean-spirited Alban Watkins -- returns to play a key role in the treasure hunt which forms one of the most comical episodes in the saga. He gets his throat cut in a terrible revenge for atrocities committed against the Irish in Australia. Then in "Rebecca and the Angels" Martha's fourth diary is found in -- of all places -- Yarra Glen in the Australian state of Victoria. Why? Well, the most obvious answer to that question is that that is the way the story came to me; but it can be no coincidence that my son Martin and his family live not far from Melbourne, and that I have made two visits to "Ned Kelly Country" and discovered a good deal about the miseries heaped upon the poor Irish immigrants -- convicts and free settlers -- in that harsh land. I have also read, and been greatly moved by, two very important books about that time and that place. One is Robert Hughes's massive tome called *The Fatal Shore*, and the other is Peter Carey's wonderful novel called *True History of the Kelly Gang*. So the detail recounted in two letters in *House of Angels* -- one from Patty on pp 273-275 and the other from "an Irish Friend" on pp 379-385 -- is based quite carefully on a well authenticated episode in the penal colonies.

The author meets Ned Kelly in Glenrowan. This little town is in the heart of bushranger country

Ireland and the Irish. This brings me to the Irish component in the stories. The Irish are not exactly everywhere, but they do pop up in all of the books, and Martha has a soft spot for them, just as I do. That should not be surprising to anybody. Ever since the Age of the Saints there has been Irish immigration into Pembrokeshire, particularly from the south-east corner of the country around Waterford and Wexford. Many Irish tribes settled in Pembrokeshire, and in some periods of local history there seem to have been more Irish here that Welsh! In the seventeenth and eighteenth centuries there was more immigration, but on a smaller scale because of mistrust between Roman Catholics and Protestants. That mistrust was certainly still present in the first half of the nineteenth century; but Irish labourers were needed at certain times of the year to help with the hay harvest and then the corn harvest. Later on more Irish families flooded through Fishguard, Cardigan and other ports, but most of them were headed for the South Wales Coalfield, enticed by the prospect of great fortunes to be made in the coal mines and in the new metal-working industries. Very few of them made great fortunes, and most ended up in urban squalor instead of the rural squalour they had left behind on the Emerald Isle. Then came the Irish Potato Famine, one of the most terrible episodes in the recorded history of these islands. It could have been managed effectively by the politicians in London, but they were in turns arrogant, complacent, devious and vindictive, and compassionate people like Martha did indeed try to help to alleviate the suffering of the poor starving peasants.

The Evangelical Revivals. Coming, as I do, from a Methodist background, I have some "inside knowledge" of nonconformity, of the yearning for personal salvation, and of the vision -- shared by many -- of a sort of Kingdom of Heaven on Earth from which sin and misery are banished and in which virtue and "plenty" bring contentment to all. My father was a Methodist local preacher who devoted his life to the Christian cause and who spent many hours of every week working for Wesley Methodist Chapel in Haverfordwest. He organized popular "singing festivals" and evangelical events in the chapel, and succeeded on many occasions in filling that huge building to overflowing. As the chapel congregation declined inexorably in the period 1960 - 1980 he longed for another great Religious Revival -- but it never came, and he went to his grave disappointed and even disillusioned. That is not to say that he was a sad or pathetic figure -- he had a great zest for life, a steadfast faith, a sharp and enquiring mind, and a wonderful sense of fun. Maybe there is something of him in the character of Amos Jones Minor Prophet! The nonconformists and the Revivals had to feature in the books, given my own personal history. My portrayal of the Baptists and

Tabernacle Chapel, Newport, first constructed in 1815 by the Calvinistic Methodists

their intolerance of human frailty may seem harsh in "Flying with Angels", but I hope that the reader will take away the message that religion is not the problem, and that the real problem of religion is the exercise of power by those who forget how to be humble.

The Dimetian Dialect. As I explain in the novels, the Dimetian Dialect really was spoken by many people in North Pembrokeshire in the centuries leading up to the time of my stories. By 1850 it was virtually extinct. It was spoken in pockets across North Pembrokeshire, from St Davids in the west to Cwm Gwaun in the east, and it differed from conventional Welsh in that it had many English "loan words" that had been "Welshified" and had certain quirks of grammar, pronunciation and spelling. Meredith Morris, a clergyman and folk tale collector who worked in the Gwaun Valley, was fascinated by this strange dialect, and actually published a small tome in 1890 with the title "A Glossary of the Dimetian Dialect of Pembrokeshire." I am unsure whether it was distinct enough from normal Welsh to be incomprehensible to a native Welsh speaker, and whether in written form it would be difficult to interpret, but giving the Dimetian Dialect to Martha as a "private language" seemed to me to be a convenient device for the protection of her most secret thoughts from those around her and from future generations!

The Importance of Small Things. And then there are the little details that a writer of historical fiction also has to get right. The minutiae of daily life in an early nineteenth-century gentry house are the things which help to give "texture" to the story and which help to pull the reader into the world imagined and created for the heroes and the villains of the tale. So I needed to know about clothes, diet, kitchen practices, gardening, animal husbandry, the conduct of cases in the petty sessions and the county courts, and even quite unusual matters like child adoption procedures.

For the climax (is that the right word?) of *On Angel Mountain* I had to know a lot about female undergarments in 1797, and thought that the best place to do my research would be the Victoria and Albert Museum. I had occasion to go to London, and called in to investigate the female dress of the time. When asked about the nature of my enquiry, I said that I wanted to know everything about lady's knickers in the last decade of the eighteenth century. The curator raised her eyebrows in surprise, but assumed that my enquiry was of an academic nature since my wife and our friend Lorna were with me at the time.

Her answer was surprising. "Oh, there weren't any," she said. "It was considered at the time that it was immoral for a lady to wear anything resembling gentlemen's breeches. So only prostitutes wore undergarments. But fashions did change, and after 1806 knickers or pantaloons did come into widespread use." That was a handy piece of information, as readers of my first novel will appreciate!

Winter on Carningli. There is a sprinkling of snow and a low sun. Newport and the estuary are in the distance

On Discovering Diaries

Many readers of the Saga have told me that their conviction that the stories are factual rather than fictional springs from the "authentic" feel which I have given to the Introductions to the five novels. Of course I tried to make them as authentic as possible -- it is a part of an author's job to make **everything** realistic and believable. In a sense, I was stuck with having to write those introductions as soon as I accepted that the novels had to be written in a diary format. I could have launched straight in on the diary entries from the first page, but then I realized that I had to set the scene somehow, and to make a link for the reader between today and yesterday. I assumed that many readers would not know the area in which the stories were set, let alone the social and historical context for Martha's life story. There would be no more reason for Martha, or anybody else writing a daily diary, to describe their familiar landscape any more than to describe their own physical appearance. So some way had to be found of describing the area around Newport and Carningli in words other than Martha's own.

When Martha's life history was "given" to me during that strange episode on Gran Canaria, I was also given the germ of an idea that her first diary was found in a box in the attic of a ruinous Plas Ingli. So I worked at it, and constructed the elaborate tale of an unnamed narrator (widely assumed to be me!) caught up in the discovery and translation of the diary volumes. That gave me the opportunity of writing what was in effect a short story (which I called a Postscript) tagged onto the front of the main novel. The device seems to have worked quite well, and some readers have told me that they enjoyed reading the modern "whodunnit" as much as, if not more than, Martha's own diary entries!

Having invented a strange mechanism for discovering the diary reproduced in *On Angel Mountain* I was stuck with that format when it came to the reproduction of the heroine's later diaries. Four more volumes to write, and four more means of discovery to be invented .... how on earth should I do it? I was not sure at the out-

48

set whether my inventiveness could rise to the challenge of keeping readers intrigued and involved, over four further books. I took the Introductions one at a time. For *House of Angels*, an old painting would trigger off the treasure hunt for the further scribblings of Mistress Martha, which would be found hidden in the library of Plas Pontfaen. Then for *Dark Angel*, how about some volumes deposited in the National Library of Wales? And where might Martha have hidden her diaries relating to the period of the Rebecca Riots? Well, she might have given them to Thomas Campbell Foster, and they might have found their way to Australia in the possession of his son who emigrated. Finally, the diaries from the end of her life -- what better thing could she have done than to give them to Bessie, her faithful maidservant and friend?

With the theme for each introduction decided, I had to do something interesting which would connect all of them together, creating in effect a group of short stories. The thrill of the hunt was one thing which might "draw in" the reader, and the translations of the diaries from the Dimetian dialect into English was another intriguing feature; but as I got to know Martha, I realized that she would have enjoyed leading her "diary hunters" a merry dance, a century and a half after her death. So I had to have her smiling down from her place among the angels, teasing and tricking the narrator as he became more and more obsessed with finding one diary after another and with learning how to read her mind. But the most important realization of all was that Abraham Jenkins should figure large in the Introductions, as an interesting and eccentric character in his own right. So I worked at developing the relationship between him and the narrator as one diary after another was discovered, and also at developing his own personal passion for Martha, given that only he could read her handwriting, see her crossings out and corrections, and see (sometimes quite literally) her blood and tears still staining those battered hand-written pages. I describe this rather strange relationship on page 19 of *Flying with Angels*. Towards the end, Abraham was not just obsessed with Martha -- he was in love with her, just like all the other men who came to know her well. So the joy and the tragedy of Abraham Jenkins became another story -- and that is why I invented the symmetry between his death and that of Mistress Martha, and why I started *Flying with Angels* with Abraham's Obituary.

It goes without saying that as one story followed another, I became quite attached to Abraham Jenkins, just as I became attached to Joseph Harries, Owain Laugharne, Wilmot Gwynne and Amos Jones. He was an invention -- but here is a confession. He was mod-

Golden evening light, Carn Edward

elled -- in a rough sort of way -- on William John Jenkins, a near neighbour of mine who lived at one time in the house now occupied by my wife and myself, and who spent the latter years of his life at Waun Isaf, on the edge of the common. He was a smallholder who kept a few sheep. He had an old and faithful sheepdog. He kept a diary himself, and was a warm, intelligent and good-humoured human being who liked nothing better than to discuss the weather and the state of the world. He was immersed in Welsh culture. Following the death of his brother Dewi, he lived alone in the cottage, and knew every stone on the south side of the mountain. I met him almost every time I climbed up those rocky slopes, and I was very fond of him. He was not in the best of health in 2005, at the time when *Flying with Angels* was published, but he kept going, as a man with animals has to do. Then in the early summer of 2006 he died, in circumstances eerily similar to those described on pages 15-17 of the book, leaving behind him an old dog, a cottage and a flock of sheep................

3. The Writing Process

They say that all art, whether great or simply workmanlike, is a product of ten per cent inspiration and ninety percent perspiration. With five connected novels now under my belt, I have to agree. It was one thing to "receive" a story complete with characters and locations, but it was quite another to get that story down in writing, in an organized and coherent form which would not just make sense to me but to readers who know nothing of the social history or the landscape of North Pembrokeshire generally and Carningli in particular. And it was more difficult again to make the story a real page turner and a best-seller.

In 1999 I had no idea how to create a novel from scratch. I was concerned at first that I had never completed -- or even started -- a creative writing course, and that I am not even a great reader of other people's novels. But then I realized that there were positives as well as negatives in my situation. For a start, I form quite strong views of the novels I do read, and I tend to analyze them quite carefully during and after the reading process. I know what I like and dislike, and I know why. I also suspect that creative writing courses encourage "formulaic" writing and the creation of novels which are targetted at particular genres or readers and even at particular publishers or newspaper literary editors! And on the basis that "one should write about what one knows", I do at least know my territory, having walked across Carningli and scrambled to its summit on innumerable occasions since moving to the area thirty years ago, in the autumn of 1976.

In 1999 a number of factors seemed to be urging me into the creation of the Angel Mountain saga:

** As day followed day, the story inside my head showed no sign of fading away, encouraging me to think that it demanded to be used.

51

**   Many years ago, as an O-level and A-level student, I enjoyed studying English literature and was lucky enough to have, in the person of Fred Nicholls, an inspirational teacher. At a tender age I discovered the pleasure of writing, and I have never had problems in putting words together in an order which seems to make sense. Neither have I ever suffered from the deadly "writer's block". If I had not become a geography lecturer and geomorphologist, I might have ended up reading for an English degree.

**   I also knew that many old friends, including Marley Davies of the Victoria Bookshop in Haverfordwest, had been pushing me for years to take up fiction writing, and had reminded me that with a faithful local readership I would probably not lose money on a novel, even if I did not make a fortune.

**   As for the publishing side of things, that held no terrors either, since I have been publishing books at the rate of one or two a year almost since the beginning of time.

With all of this in mind, I decided that I might as well get stuck in.

My Five P's

I worked out from the very beginning, as an amateur novelist, that I needed to consider **people, place, pace, plot and purpose**.   These became my "five P's" which had to be kept in mind at all times during the writing process.

People. Novels are essentially about people, their relationships and their reactions to unusual situations. At the outset, I did have concerns about my ability to "fashion" the characters in the story and to describe them in a way which would attract the empathy of the reader. When I read novels myself, I want to "like" the characters, both villains and heroes, and I want them to be sufficiently well-drawn for me to create mental pictures of them. If action dominates a book to the extent of squeezing out the portrayal of those caught up in it (as in *The Da Vinci Code*) I find that I am ultimately not satisfied or convinced by it. So I had to work hard at character portrayal, both through descriptions of facial features and clothes and through conversations and actions. But there are more than 200 characters in the whole saga, and early on I had to come to terms with the fact that while some might be portrayed in depth, many others would be sketchy and even shadowy figures. I did not always get things right; for example, I still regret that I did not develop David's character more, given the fact that as Martha's husband and the father of her children, he figures strongly in the story even after his death. But there are some characters with whom I am reasonably content: for example Bessie the maid, Joseph Harries the Wizard, Grandpa Isaac and Grandma Jane, Patty the prostitute, servants Billy, Will and Shemi, the poetic and romantic Owain Laugharne, the tragic figure of Iestyn Price, the villainous Moses Lloyd, and in the later novels Hugh Williams, George Price, Amos Jones and Wilmot Gwynne. Among Martha's children, the characters of Brynach and Daisy are developed more fully than those of Dewi, Betsi and Sara. The reader's impression of all of them is of course conditioned by the manner in which Martha describes them and by the extent to which she loves them, needs them or despises them. So the portraits are anything but balanced -- and that's the way it is in real life.

Place. In a sense, this was the easiest aspect of the story to deal with. As a geographer by training I have a well-developed sense of place, an eye for landscape details and some understanding of what marks out the landscape of Carningli and North Pembrokeshire as being different from other landscapes. But I had to rein in my instinct for describing landscape, on the grounds that my fascination with it is not necessarily matched by that of the reader! Having wandered around Cilgwyn and Carningli for thirty years or so, I know almost every nook and cranny of this beloved landscape, and I have tried to give Martha the same sense of "belonging" that I feel myself. She loves the mountain and all its moods almost as dearly as she loves life itself. She feels that the mountain is a part of her, and that she is a part of the mountain. In her relationship with Carningli and the Plas, she illustrates, as perfectly as I can manage it, what the Welsh word *hiraeth* means -- longing, belonging and loving a piece of

Martha's country -- Carningli and the common, with Newport in the foreground

land, whether inherited or adopted. That is not a peculiarly Celtic thing, but the link between land and people is undoubtedly very strong in Wales, as almost every Welsh writer has recognized. Because Martha loves her home territory so much it is, I hope, natural for her to describe in the pages of her diary what happens to the sky and the land when there is a thunder-storm, or a torrential deluge, or a heavy snowfall. It is also quite natural for her to gasp in wonderment when she sees the abundant bird life on the cliffs between Newport and Cwm yr Eglwys, or when she wades through an early summer meadow full of flowers and herbs, or when she sees the lengthening shadows of evening among the summit crags. At intervals in all of the novels I have been at pains to describe -- briefly -- "the land" in some of its moods, as a counterbalance to the heavy or dramatic episodes which hit poor Martha between the eyes with alarming frequency! All five of the Angel Mountain novels are "regional novels", rooted in a place which is well known to most of the early readers of the books. The early marketing and publicity efforts for the series were directed primarily at Pembrokeshire people but also readers who know and love North Pembrokeshire as a holiday destination. I was confident that the readers of the books would like the locations, and much less confident that they would like Mistress Martha!

Pace. Some authors, Dan Brown included, drive a story forward so relentlessly that there is only one gear -- superdrive. It has worked for him, but the story that came to me had a good deal of quietness in it, and so there had to be many tranquil episodes. There also had to be time for character development and for the exploration of personal relationships. But I also had to pack in many violent action episodes. So I tried to develop a wave-like structure on the way to the book's climax, with action-packed episodes interspersed with quiet ones in which I develop the characters through their involvement in local traditions or in domestic activities. There is nothing new about this, and writers and musicians have realized over the centuries that on the way to the climax of a piece andante needs to follow allegro, and vice versa. But each wave needs to be a little higher than the last, and the last wave is the one that crashes onto the shore with the greatest force, bringing the piece to an end. All perfectly sensible -- but then I realized that the first part of the story in my head (in *On Angel Mountain*) had a "double whammy" climax, and I accepted that from a technical point of view it was not a bad idea to have **two** massive waves at the end, with the final one arriving out of the blue just when the reader thinks that the story is all over! Readers told me that it worked for the first novel in the series, and so I continued the tradition in the other four as well.

Plot. Each one of the five novels has a complex plot, given to me in considerable detail during that strange night of delirium in 1999. That is not to say that all was decided in advance, and that no "manufacturing" was needed. In fact a good deal of tweaking and reorganizing had to be done, and various episodes that were fixed in my head had to be dumped because they did not fit into the main story-line as it was developing. Stories can become too complex, and there is then the risk of leaving the reader behind as the twists and turns become ever more convoluted. Think of Wilkie Collins' *The Woman in White*! Various other episodes had to be changed during the writing process because Mistress Martha did not approve of the direction in which I wanted to take her. So there was some scrapping and rewriting of sections -- and in retrospect the reason was almost always that I wanted Martha to do something that would have been out of character. Experienced authors say that their characters and stories take on a life and a momentum of their own, and that it is unwise to resist the route that they choose to take. I think I now know what that means. In each of the novels, several story-lines are interwoven, and that involved a lot of careful planning and hard work on my part. In a sense, the simplest stories are in *On Angel Mountain* and *Rebecca and the Angels* -- but even here there is more going on than might meet the eye, with an adventure story running in parallel with other stories and mysteries relating to Martha's family and friends and to her sexual adventures. The darkest story-line is in *Dark Angel*, where Martha reveals her insecurity and her paranoia while at the same time showing her compassion and her devotion to her family. By far the most complex story -- and the one which gave me the greatest pleasure as a writer -- is "House of Angels", which weaves together five different story-lines.

Purpose.   The most important part of the unwritten contract between writer and reader is the bit that says that the writer must entertain. In historical fiction the writer should educate as well, giving the reader a glimpse of another world long gone. That glimpse should be reasonably accurate and authentic, but not too slavishly based upon "the truth." If a writer can evoke the sights and smells of the time, and the feeling of what life must have been like for heroes, villains and other characters, so much the better. And as I have said, for a geographer like me, the building up of a "sense of place" is very important indeed. But if novels are really about ordinary people in extraordinary situations, a novelist has to concentrate very hard on character, characteristics, appearance and personal relationships. On almost every page of a novel there is a developing relationship between one character and another, and therein lies the challenge for the writer and the excitement for the reader. But through the welter of events and personal interactions something else has to be visible -- namely the author's "take" on life. So what is my take on life, and what am I really trying to do in the novels? Many readers have said to me as they have worked their way through the saga "Poor Martha! Why does she have to suffer so much? And when will she really find true happiness?" One of my readers got so upset with what Martha was having to put up with that she went up to Plas Ingli to pray for her, in the hope that she might find peace. Well, my heroine does have to put up with a great deal of brutality, suffering and prejudice, and she does meet some very unpleasant people, and she does lose almost all of those whom she loves in the most appalling of circumstances. She seems to weep more frequently than she laughs. But here is a gentle reminder for readers -- remember that the novels give brief "snapshots" of her life, and that there are long periods which I have not written about at all. Let us imagine that those periods were happy, and mundane, and maybe even boring -- and maybe therefore not very interesting to the reader or to the author! I am sure that Mistress Martha had her good times as a wife, as a mother, and as a merry widow. Conjure those episodes up for yourself, if you will! Then you can try to understand my real purpose in writing the saga, which I am now beginning to clarify for myself. Whatever happens to her, she grits her teeth and fights back. She even fights her way out of the miseries associated with miscarriage, the murder of a husband, or the loss of a child. When she is plunged into the dark horrors of depression, she fights her way back into the bright light of a spring morning -- and she does this more than once. So while I am trying to describe a set of characters in a rough landscape and a rough time, and while I am trying to improve my own understanding of the human condition, I am also doing something which is ultimately life-affirming. The books are actually quite "moral" in the sense that virtue and depravity are both rewarded in appropriate ways. The wicked are punished, and the good are rewarded -- maybe not instantly, but all in good time. Since I was a young man, I have had unbounded admiration for people who have the capacity to cope with whatever life throws at them -- sometimes with quiet stoicism and sometimes with flames in their eyes and iron in their sinews. Of course I love Martha and many of the other characters to whom I have given life, but in writing about them I suppose what I have really been doing is composing a hymn to the human spirit.

The Diary Format

Once I got into the swing of things, I discovered that the **diary format** was ideal (thanks, Martha!) for easy reading, with short snippets of text suitable for reading in bed before nodding off! Also, by quoting from a diary I could give the story some very rapid changes of mood, with Martha up one day and down the next, changing her mind and her view of the world -- and even her opinion of her husband -- on an almost daily basis. That suited her somewhat erratic temperament. One cannot get that sort of immediacy with a third-person narrative, which is generally full of predictions and anticipations -- and author's analyses (think of Hardy's *Tess of the D'Urbervilles*). I wanted to create lively and well-rounded characters, a strong sense of place, and an urgent story-line within the story as it had been "given" to me. But the diary format also presented me with three great difficulties. The first was that Martha had to be portrayed for the reader not by an impartial narrator but by Martha herself. So it would not have been appropriate anywhere for her to describe herself as a stunningly beautiful woman, or even as sexy or desirable. She would not even have described her own figure, or eye colour, or hair, in the pages of her own diary.

So I had to find ways of portraying her through other people's words, remembered and recorded in the diary. That was difficult --

but I realised that there was no harm in leaving the physical descriptions of her in a somewhat sketchy state, allowing every reader to imagine a slightly different Martha Morgan! Second, a young woman writing in her diary would not naturally indulge in grand phrases or purple prose when describing sunsets or scenery or even dramatic events. So over and again I had to rein in my artistic instincts and keep descriptions sparse when I wanted to indulge myself and the reader. And third, I had to find a way of making Martha sound like a naive teenager in the opening pages of *On Angel Mountain* and to develop her writing style as she matured to being a competent mother and estate manager in *House of Angels* and eventually to being a matriarchal and world-weary figure at the end of *Flying with Angels*. That actually was less troublesome than it might appear, since I dare say I matured as a writer as Martha matured over the passage of almost sixty years of her life!

Getting Words onto Paper

I find the process of writing quite easy. I can write almost anywhere, so long as I have my lap-top with me, and a few essential reference books. It doesn't seem to worry me too much if there are lots of other things going on in life. I frequently stop work for a few days or weeks, and pick up where I left off. No garden shed purdah for me!! As noted above, I haven't yet suffered from writer's block, but maybe that is because I had no need to manufacture my story as I go along -- it was all there, in my head. The first book took me 18 months to write, but that was largely because I had a lot of background research to do. Also, I was very apprehensive about the quality of my writing, and kept on revising bits of text. In the end, I discovered that I was making things worse rather than better, and losing spontaneity. For the other 4 books I settled into a steady routine -- 4 months of writing, 4 months of editing / refereeing / production, and 4 months of publicity / marketing / thinking about the next book. So each year was split into three segments; the edges between them were rather blurred at times, but I never lost sight of them. When I am in the mood, I write very fast, and if I am into a particularly difficult scene, dealing with death or sex for example, I may write for 12 hours or so, and not stop until it is finished. My average output is maybe 5,000 words a day -- some days I may write more than 10,000.

Old cannon on Fishguard's Market Square, with the Royal Oak Inn behind. Since the events of the last Invasion are well known, historical accuracy was important when describing David's role in defeating the enemy!

The key to each story is in the paperwork which I assemble in advance. First there is the synopsis, which I develop quite fully before I start writing the text. I begin with a brief summary of maybe three or four pages, outlining the main components in the story, the timeline, and the section or chapter headings. Once I am reasonably happy with that, I develop the synopsis, expanding it to maybe 15 pages and including considerable detail and maybe even pieces of narrative or conversations which I may later actually use in the manuscript. But I do not necessarily treat the synopsis with great respect, and as indicated above, once the story starts to take on a life of its own it may lead me into all sorts of avenues that I have never previously visited. So whole chunks of my synopsis may end up in the bin, or at least drastically revised.

The second piece of paperwork is the full character list for the book on which I am working, including names, dates of birth and death, places of residence, and family relationships (husbands, wives, parents, children and so forth) for everybody appearing in the story. That is where the modern computer's "cut and paste" facility comes in very handy, since most of these character entries can be taken from my cumulative character list and put back into it when the manuscript of a particular book is finished. I admit to not being as organized on the matter of "bit players" as I should be, and some readers may have noticed inconsistencies as to the places of residence, age and appearance of certain characters between one book and the next! That's where copy editors and proof readers come in handy, if you can afford them. My wife has done stirling work on checking continuity and characters, but she has her own life to lead and her own job to do in the Candle Workshop, so she cannot be involved all of the time.........

The third piece of paperwork is the list of diary entries, which I update as carefully as I can, adding to it day by day as one piece of text after another comes off the production line. This list is more important than one might imagine, because it is crucial for birthdays and wedding anniversaries, dates of deaths, and dates of great events such as the French Invasion, the first episode of gate burning in the Rebecca Riots, and even for authenticity when it comes to annual festivals and *cnapan* contests! There have been many occasions during the writing of the books when I have had to revisit the sequences and the dates of diary entries and make quite substantial adjustments. Sometimes I have had to roll diary entries together so as to prevent the text becoming too staccato; and on other occasions I have made entries very short and sparse for dramatic effect.

I work straight onto the computer, although I may sometimes make hand-written notes (in the middle of the night, maybe, if a sudden inspiration comes into my head) which I will then use as the basis for a conversation or an action episode. My father was an ace two-fingered typist, and as a child I can remember him banging away on his old cast-iron typewriter at a speed which I thought mightily impressive. He used his two index fingers and nothing else. Maybe it's in the genes, but I have followed exactly his way of doing things -- although it has to be said that a modern computer keyboard is a great deal easier to use than that of a chunky 1940's manual machine! When I am writing, I look at my fingers and the keyboard rather than the computer screen, so I do make lots of mistakes. But that doesn't matter. I correct and edit as I go along, and then I review everything at the end of each writing session. Every day, while I am writing, Inger pops in every now and then to urge me to write faster or to get out and have some fresh air, and every evening she insists on reading the day's output before going to sleep. Sometimes I refuse to let her see it, if I am still unhappy with what I have written, or if an episode is still incomplete. But when she has read each piece, and given me her comments, I make adjustments (if I agree with what she is saying!) and that's it. After that, I change hardly anything. Not for me are the four, five, six versions of a manuscript, stretching over months and years of fiddling! I prefer to keep a high level of spontaneity in my writing -- which is entirely appropriate for a diary which is nothing if it cannot be immediate, honest and "natural".

Once the manuscript is complete, I work out where the natural break points are, and then divide the text up into manageable chunks -- sections and chapters. Then I might do a small amount of tweaking, cutting out repetitions or things that sit awkwardly. But I don't deliberately cut the text down to a certain length. It so happened that I needed 145,000 words to tell *On Angel Mountain*, but 185,000 words, give or take a few, to tell each of the next three stories, which are all more complex. For *Flying with Angels*, I needed 175,000 words to tell the story. Once the bits and pieces of manuscript are assembled into one place, and once I have thrown out the oldest versions of my chapters and cleaned up my desktop, I work on a rough book design on an A4 format and print out half a dozen copies of the full draft. Now it begins to look like a book! I use a great deal of paper, and a lot of printer ink, and a lot of time, in that particular exercise. Space is needed on the pages for comments and corrections. Then off go the bulky folders to my six referees, who generally take 2 - 4 weeks to read them. They are crucial cogs in the publishing machinery, and I am eternally grateful to them for being both diligent and honest! They pick up many things which Inger and I have missed -- spelling mistakes, spacing and punctuation errors, anachronisms, and characters who are balder, shorter, younger or slimmer than they were in the previous volume, or who may be simply living in the wrong place. They also comment on the pace of the story, tell me when things are dragging, and often get very irritated with Mistress Martha for failing to realize that somebody or other is desperately in love with her. Some of their comments are complimentary, and others are not -- which is as it should be. Then I talk to my referees, go through all six of the annotated drafts together, and work out whether I agree or disagree with what has been written in the margins. I have no qualms about accepting suggestions for improvements, and am not so precious about my text as to resent suggested alterations or improvements. Sometimes one person's comments will be cancelled out by another person's. One referee may say "This page is far too slow -- speed it up!" and another will say about the same piece of text "I loved the gentle pace of this page -- more like it, please!" So I make more corrections, and the book is almost as I want it to be.

The final bits of tweaking are done not with my editorial hat on my head, but my design hat. To make the book ready for the printer, I have to reduce it from an A4 format to an A5 format, with headers and page numbers added. I put in the ornaments at the end of each diary entry. I add the front matter and back matter (title page, contents, map, acknowledgments etc) and only then do I discover how many pages I need for the printed and published book. I try and aim for a multiple of sixteen, since that makes for better printing economics. I go through the whole thing, page by page, to ensure that the book looks good. For example, one needs the diary date headers to be at the top of a page if possible, or the middle of a

*Old buildings in the Pontfaen farmyard.
I imagine that those of Plas Ingli will
have looked like this*

page maybe, but never on the last line! And one cannot have the last word of a paragraph spilling over from one page to another. Sometimes paragraphs have to be shortened or even split in order to get page layouts looking good. When that is all done, and I am reasonably happy with the "look" of the book, I check the pagination again, and may have to lose a few pages in order to get to a multiple of sixteen. A lot of lines (and a lot of space) can be saved by looking at paragraphs which have just one or two words on their last lines. If one shortens those paragraphs just a little, the text hops up and gives you a final line which is a long one. If you do that often enough, through a whole chapter or even through a whole book, you save maybe ten pages.

At last, everything is ready, with the text looking as perfect as it ever will be. In a perfect world of modern computers, you save everything on PDF files (in effect, giving a "photograph of each page) and send those files off as Email attachments or on disk to the printer. He checks that there are no formatting problems, and then feeds the whole lot into his computer. The computer feeds the book on into the printing press, and 2,000 (or 3,000, or whatever) copies magically appear, to be delivered at your front door on pallets a few days later! That's the theory anyway. It worked for the very last book of the Saga, because I had the right technology; but for the other books I could not make PDF files that were completely compatible with the systems used by the printer, so I had to print off best-quality copies of each book, page by page, so that he could scan them in and make his own camera-ready copy or CRC. That was very slow and very boring, and I will not test your patience by describing it any further..........

Influences

Authors are influenced by a host of different things -- books and films, family dynamics, lifetime experiences, teachers and friends, and even their state of health and the weather! In trying to work out what has influenced me, it has to be true that *everything* has. My own education, for a start. And in that, I was lucky, with teachers from an early age who taught me to see beauty in the world, to observe carefully, to work hard and play hard, and to take pleasure in creating things. Having not really done any creative writing for 50 years, since I did my English "A" level, writing *On Angel Mountain* was an adventure. At Haverfordwest Grammar School I had a very exciting and inspiring teacher -- Fred Nicholls. He now lives in Newport, and is one of my referees. He read several of the pre-publication drafts of the novels, and at the end of it all he was still -- as in 1956 -- putting me right on anachronisms, grammatical errors and awkward phraseology!!

What about books which have made a deep impression on me? I do not read a lot of fiction, but books that do spring to mind as being mightily impressive include *True History of the Kelly* Gang (Peter Carey), *Cold Mountain* (Charles Frasier), *The Shipping News* (Annie Proulx), *On the Black Hill* (Bruce Chatwin), *How Green was my Valley*

(Richard Llewellyn), *Heart of Darkness* (Joseph Conrad), *The Cruel Sea* (Nicholas Monsarrat), *Schindler's List* (Thomas Keneally), *The Clan of the Cave Bear* (Jean Auel), *Crow Road* (Iain Banks), *Thank you, Jeeves* (PG Wodehouse), *Pride and Prejudice* (Jane Austen), *To Kill a Mockingbird* (Harper Lee), *The Valley of Fear* (Arthur Conan Doyle), *Hosts of Rebecca* (Alexander Cordell), *These is my Words* (Nancy Turner), and *The Unforgiving Wind* (John Harris). There. That tells you something about my taste in fiction, but what else it tells you I am not sure!

And novels I have not liked or have been unable to finish? These come to mind: *Wuthering Heights* (Emily Bronte), *Ross Poldark* (Winston Graham), *Angela's Ashes* (Frank McCourt), *Aberystwyth Mon Amour* (Malcolm Pryce), *The No 1 Ladies' Detective Agency* (Alexander McCall Smith), *The Poisonwood Bible* (Barbara Kingsolver), *The Lord of the Rings* (JRR Tolkien), *Captain Corelli's Mandolin* (Louis de Bernieres) (which I once heard described by a lady on a train as Captain Cornetto's Mandarin), *The English Passengers* (Matthew Kneale), *People of the Black Mountains* (Raymond Williams), *Feet in Chains* (Kate Roberts), and everything by Agatha Christie, Ian Fleming, Jeffrey Archer, and a good many others besides. I am not saying that these are bad novels, but that they simply did not "pull me in" and transport me into other worlds.

I have to say something about Lewis Grassic Gibbon and *A Scots Quair*. There are three volumes, called *Sunset Song, Cloud Howe* and *Grey Granite*. The first one is particularly impressive -- once one has got used to the strange language used by the author -- and I am convinced that Dylan Thomas got his inspiration for *Under Milk Wood* from the quirky and wonderful opening chapter. It is labelled as a Prelude, with the title "The Unfurrowed Field." The stories describe three phases in the life of the heroine, Chris Guthrie, who is essentially a peasant and a victim of circumstance. She is an opportunist too, when survival depends on it, but she never abandons her peasant mentality, and her attitudes bring into mind those of the tragic peasant villains in *Jean de Florette* by Marcel Pagnol. I think my books are lighter and more positive than those of Grassic Gibbon, with much more complex story-lines and (I think!) more likable characters. Other readers have compared my books with Hardy's *Tess of the D'Urbervilles* and with Wilkie Collins' *The Woman in White*. I am flattered! Not that I like *Tess* very much -- I find it pretentious and turgid in places, with many of the key events being so absurd as to be unbelievable. But Wilkie Collins I greatly admire -- especially his ability to hold in his head a myriad of plotting complexities while keeping the reader guessing, page after page, as to what is actually going on. He was a much better storyteller than Dan Brown, if I may be so bold, because he knew how to portray character and gave himself the space to do it ....

My Favourite Bits

I am often asked which bits of the Saga have given me the most pleasure as a writer. I suppose that people are really asking which bits have been the most difficult to write, technically, and which bits

One of the little caves on Carningli

have "drawn me in" emotionally and left me somewhat drained. Technically, the book which has given me most satisfaction is *House of Angels*, because I think it has hardly any spare fat on its bones, and because I had to work really hard at weaving together five different story strands without losing sight of any of them. What are those five strands? Ah, that would be telling!

From the point of view of emotional involvement, my favourite is undoubtedly *Flying with Angels*, in which Martha grows old. Like Martha, I am coming to terms with the fact that the body slows down, while the mind revisits (more and more frequently!) the good old days long gone; and like Martha, I have to realise that I am not immortal. So the idea of Martha having one last fling, and growing old disgracefully, is something that all elderly people can relate to. I think there might be more of me in this book than in any of the others. The tragedy of Amos Jones and his church meant a lot to me, and I put much hard work into the theme of "letting go". At the end of it all, with Martha asleep on the summit of her blessed mountain, I felt that I could let go of her, and let her rest in peace. Does that sound sentimental and silly? So be it -- authors can be sentimental just like everybody else...........

My favourite bits? Not too difficult. Here goes:

Martha's miscarriage, on pp 56 - 59 of *On Angel Mountain* -- and the description of her subsequent recovery. How on earth could a man dare to write about such a thing from a woman's perspective? How indeed? But I tried, and for a novice novelist it was a serious and emotional task.

The Confession of Eli Davids, on pp 241-245 of *On Angel Mountain*. I don't know why, but I am very fond of this little piece of text. I wrote it very quickly, but it left me drained. At the end of it, Martha says "I must stop. Perhaps, if I have the strength, I will write more tomorrow." That was me speaking, not Mistress Martha.

The final confrontation between Martha and Moses in the cave, on pp 310-323 of *On Angel Mountain*. That was very tough to write, and in one quite extended scene I had to keep up the tension, imply Moses's madness, and draw together all the loose threads of the story. I also had to be very careful not to overstep the mark with respect to explicit sex or gratuitous violence. I had to work hard to ensure that I could never be accused of straying into pornography.

The disappearance and finding of Daisy, on pp 211-218 of *House of Angels*. This gave me the opportunity to try and describe every mother's worst nightmare, and to demonstrate the strength and devotion of Martha's family and servants.

The scene in which Martha watches Owain in the pool at Pandy, on pp 222-225 of *House of Angels*.

Martha's "Testament to Beauty" on pp 189-200 of *Dark Angel*. This was tough to write -- funny, tender, and passionate. I had to try and portray Martha's apprehension (rather like that of a teenager on her first serious date) and Owain's personal conflict between expressing his love for Martha and behaving with sensitivity. The

Capel Brynberian as it appears today

whole episode is something of a disaster for both of them, but Martha comes out of it with her love and respect for Owain intact and even increased.

The discovery of the corpse of Mary Roberts on pp 244-250 of *Flying with Angels*. A very grotesque and unsettling episode, and again I had to handle it with great care. It was important to get it right, given the frivolous material contained in the previous section of the book.

And my favourite funny bits? Undoubtedly these:

The Battle of Parc Haidd, on pp 341-345 of *House of Angels*, in which a group of muscular men with very small brains make fools of themselves by digging a hole in a field looking for a non-existent treasure. The whole scene is wildly over the top, but I wanted something frothy and eccentric as a counterbalance to the brutality that exists elsewhere in the book, including the letter from "An Irish Friend" which follows on pp 379-385.

Martha's theological discussion with Rector Devonald on pp 50-56 of *Dark Angel*, during which she gets him to agree to a church wedding for Patty and Jake.

The episode relating to the loss of Martha's ugly chest following a distraint order, on pp 120-123 of *Rebecca and the Angels*, and the subsequent return of the chest by the *Ceffyl Pren* mob, described on pp 135-137.

The episode in which Martha seduces Amos Jones in Tycanol Woods, recounted on pp 185-196 of *Flying with Angels*. The seduction of a married minister of religion may not strike the reader as funny -- but I enjoyed writing this episode, trying to make it gentle, poignant and funny at the same time.

The Big Meeting in Brynberian Chapel, recounted on pp 217-226 of *Flying with Angels*, in which Shemi rescues Amos from excommunication.

The episode in which Shemi deals with the charge of murder brought against him in the Petty Sessions, on pp 238-243 of *Flying with Angels*.

4. Carn Ingli, Plas Ingli and other places

I am a Geographer by training, and since childhood I have had a very strong "sense of place" and a strong sense of belonging. My own roots are really in Haverfordwest, where I spent all of my time up to the age of 19, when I went off to college in Oxford. I still feel that a part of me is there. Another part dwells in County Durham, where Inger and I lived for eleven happy years with our two sons Stephen and Martin, in a rambling old house deep in the countryside. Other fragments are in Sweden and on Gran Canaria, and even in the outer fringes of Melbourne in Australia, for family reasons. But most of me remains here, on and around the stony slopes of Carningli.

Carningli in its August finery

I see the portrayal of places, and the creation of a "sense of place" as one of the key tasks of the novelist. Jane Austen could not really be bothered with it, but Emily Bronte created a wonderful atmosphere in *Wuthering Heights* even if other aspects of the novel are, from my perspective, grotesque and highly unsatisfactory. Peter Carey does "place" very well, as did Bruce Chatwin. I like the idea of places becoming, in effect, characters in the story, and I am attracted by the thought that if key places are described well, and in some detail, and revisited and described in monochrome here and technicolour there, readers will come to love them or hate them as they might love and hate heroes and villains. So what of these key places?

Carningli

The little mountain of Carningli dominates the landscape around Newport and Cilgwyn, and although it is only 347m (1,138 feet) high it is visible as a prominent feature from the north and east, and even from the south, for travellers approaching from Mynydd Preseli.   From certain directions, the mountain looks like a volcanic peak -- and this is appropriate, since it is indeed an ancient volcano. But it is around 450 million years old, and its present-day profile gives us little guidance as to what it looked like when it was erupt-

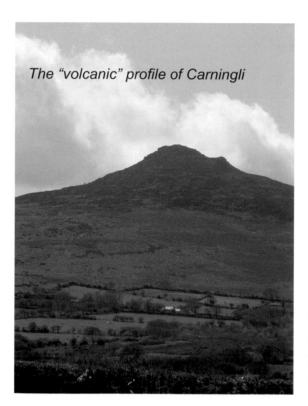

The "volcanic" profile of Carningli

ing.   When the mountain was born, the area which we currently call North Pembrokeshire was part of a great ocean, the bed of which was buckled up and down and shattered by earth movements and mountain building over millions of years. There was virtually no life on land, and very little in the sea. We know that there were tens if not hundreds of volcanoes across a wide area, since dolerites and other volcanic rocks occur in virtually all of the high points of the landscape.

When the Carningli eruption came to an end, the volcanic island immediately started to be whittled away by wave action, wind and running water. The land surface, originally many thousands of feet above its present position, was lowered inexorably by erosion, so that what we see today is essentially the "core" of the original mountain, made largely of a very hard blue-grey rock called dolerite. Some of it is "spotted dolerite" like the famous bluestone of Carn Meini.

During the Ice Age the mountain was completely covered by the ice of the massive Irish Sea Glacier, moving down from the north

Frost-shattered rock (scree) on the south face of the mountain

and north-west, possibly in several different glacial episodes. Some traces of ice erosion can still be seen on rocky slabs near the summit and on the eastern flank of the mountain. In the last glacial episode the glacier may not have over-ridden the summit, but it pressed against the northern slopes and probably into the amphitheatre of

Cilgwyn, leaving the southern and eastern slopes to be afflicted by thousands of years of frost shattering. That is why the east face of Carningli is almost obliterated by a great bank of scree even today. Martha and her children loved to climb on the great jumble of boulders and craggy outcrops, and somewhere, in the middle of it all, is Martha's cave and the crevice into which she dumped Moses Lloyd's body.

The summit of the mountain is protected in part by a splendid defensive embankment, now somewhat ruinous but still obvious to

Defensive embankment at the northern end of the Iron Age settlement on Carningli

all who climb up from the north or west. In its heyday it was probably about 10 feet high, with a vertical outward face, and maybe even a timber palisade on top. When you climb up from the east (for example, from the car-park on the Dolrannog Road) the embankment is not so obvious; that is because the scree slopes provided good natural defences for the inhabitants of the mountain against marauding warriors. So the embankment never did enclose the whole of the summit. There was a fortified village here, aligned more or less SW-NE, with three segments. The builders knew all about military architecture, and in some ways it was just as sophisticated as that of the Normans who followed maybe 2,000 years later.

In the south-west is the outer enclosure, approached through a fine gateway passage with flanking walls from what is now the open common. Animals may have been brought into this flattish area at times of trouble. Then there is a "cross wall" with a gateway in it, which separates the outer enclosure from the "inner bailey". This area encloses the three inhospitable craggy summits of the mountain; here there might have been some crude shelters against the rock faces, but the inhabitants would only have used it in times of great crisis. Then, on the north-eastern side of the mountain (on the lee side, away from the prevailing wind), there are two natural platforms on which we can still see hut circles and small enclosures. This was the main living area, and archaeologists think there may have been about 25 houses here, providing shelter for 150 people. These houses would **not** have looked

Remains of an Iron Age shelter on the flank of Carningli

like the reconstructed round houses of Castell Henllys! Here it was far too exposed for such exotic structures to survive, and so we are talking about very crude shelters, partly excavated into the stony ground and roofed over with a low lattice of branches, thatch and animal skins. Possibly these "houses" were so low and primitive that it was not even possible to stand up inside them. This living area is actually enclosed by defensive walls on three sides. Altogether there are nine entrances through the main defensive embankment.

Gates are always vulnerable, and this leads archaeologists to think that those who lived here were not particularly threatened by enemy tribes.

On both the western and eastern sides of the mountain, outside the main defended area, there are scores of embankments, paddocks and the remains of other shelters which must have been used in the pastoral and farming economy, for keeping sheep, cattle and goats and for growing and storing human food supplies and fodder. These features are all prominent, except at the height of summer when the bracken is high. The most prominent features of all are two gigantic looped banks on the eastern side of the mountain at the foot of the scree slope.

Who built the Carningli hillfort? In Martha's day most people simply assumed that "The Ancient Druids" built almost all of the old man-made features in the landscape, some time after Noah's Flood had obliterated everything. Now we know that the Carningli village was occupied during the Iron Age -- but we still do not know for sure whether it was a permanent settlement, or one that was simply occupied during the summer season by people who spent their winters in the sheltered woodlands of the river valleys. The site has never been properly excavated, so there are very few clues to be interpreted. There are some old records which suggest that the mountain was occupied by vagrants and travellers well into the Middle Ages and maybe even later, and at the other end of the scale it is now suggested that the earliest occupants may well have been here during the Bronze Age around 3,000 years ago or possibly even in the Neolithic, more than 4,000 years ago. So some of the stone walls around the summit may be older than the pyramids of Egypt, and the site may have been occupied (intermittently) by many different groups of people over something like 3,500 years.

With such a history of settlement, perhaps we should not be surprised that the mountain has been thought of as a "sacred mountain" for a very long time. There are no burials on the summit (although there may well have been human sacrifices and executions, given that the Iron Age was a pretty brutal time), so Carningli may not have been thought of as a particularly sacred or spiritual place in pre-Christian times. But when St Brynach, our local saint, came into the district around 450 AD to convert the heathen and to found his monastery at Nevern, we learn from the old texts that he was instantly attracted to the mountain. When life at the monastery became too frantic (it was, after all, on the pilgrim route to St Davids) he used to climb up onto the summit in order to "commune with the angels." That was one way of saying that he went to find solitude, to fast, and to spend time in contemplation and prayer. It may be that during the Age of the Saints the mountain acquired the name "Mons Angelorum", and it was still called this in educated circles around the year 1600. The name "Carningli" is difficult to translate, but in old Welsh it may well mean "Mount of the Angels" -- and on old maps it is called Carn Yengly or Carnengli, which are probably both corruptions of Carn Engylau.

So where does this aura of sanctity come from? Well, all who climb onto the summit know that is a very special place -- high

The grassy patch on the summit of Carningli, where St Brynach is reputed to have communed with the angels

enough above the surrounding countryside to be closer to heaven than everywhere else, low enough to be easily accessible to those who are reasonably fit, and not quite rocky enough to be dangerous or threatening. When you are on the mountain by yourself you can look down on the world with nothing but the whisper of the wind and the song of the skylarks in your ears, while you watch, far below, the bustle of Newport and the traffic speeding along the Fishguard - Cardigan road. Peace and quiet, only thirty minutes' climb from the town centre. Even today, the place is sacred.

In the stories, Martha taps into the sanctity of the place just as I do on every visit and just as thousands of others do. But note that in the stories Martha is the only one who looks on Carningli as her cathedral --- her children look on the place as a playground and as somewhere to have adventures, and the servants at the Plas look on it as a place which provides shelter from the northerly winds and which conversely endangers grazing animals. Martha's "special relationship" with the mountain is important as a storytelling device -- to enhance the "sense of place" in the Saga, and also to show that Martha is a very spiritual person although she may not be "religious." Nowadays the mountain is widely used for worship and for rituals. It is a common thing for people who love the mountain to ask that their ashes should be scattered from the summit when they die -- and their surviving relatives are very willing to oblige. I have often seen bunches of flowers, ribbons and other keepsakes or personal momentos on the summit-- and I can only assume that people use the mountain for prayers, for those who are ill or troubled, in exactly the same way as the people of Ireland use their roadside shrines. Some people who are into witchcraft use the mountain, as do the adherents of other religions including Buddhism.

Then there is the shape of the mountain. It has to be female, just as the spirit of the mountain is female. When you look at Carningli from the south or south-east, it has the unmistakable skyline profile of a woman lying on her back. To the left you see the head, with a strong forehead, and then the prominent breast and rib cage, and finally to the right the raised knees. Some people think that the reclining figure is pregnant, but that depends on your viewpoint. Perhaps the profile helps to explain the sanctity of the mountain, and author and long-distance walker Lawrence Main thinks that the summit of the mountain is on an ancient "spirit path" and is also a manifestation of the Earth Goddess. Lawrence believes that Carningli is not just a goddess but also a sleeping giant, which makes the

The profile of the mountain from the south. With the eye of faith, you can see a woman lying on her back -- head to the left, then breast, rib cage, stomach and raised knees

mountain a place of great spiritual power. He calls her Rhiannon. Lawrence claims to have spent over 700 nights on Carningli since 1995, sometimes in a tent and sometimes in the open. He is very attuned to the presence of angels on the mountain, and for some years he has conducted "dreaming experiments" with volunteers on the green patch adjacent to the summit, using the early Celtic tradition that the earth remembers everything and speaks through the dreamer. The theory is that those who are chosen will dream of angels when they sleep on the green patch which is the navel of the Earth Goddess. Not everybody who sleeps there does dream of angels, and not everybody finds it easy to identify with Lawrence's ideas, but we all have our own realities, and I am more than a little intrigued that when the story of Martha Morgan came into my head in 1999 I knew that she would die on the mountain summit. So when I came to write the final chapter of Flying with Angels it was entirely natural that she should die in exactly the same position, lying on her back, at peace beneath the frosty stars.

So are Martha and Rhiannon one and the same? Lawrence talks of the Earth Goddess, while others, who are not into goddesses and angels, refer to Martha as "Mother Wales." Has the story of Martha been given to me by Rhiannon or by the spirit of the mountain? Now there's an interesting thought.........

There are many records of strange phenomena on Carningli, and these perhaps help to explain why the mountain is deemed to be sacred. Two or three of my acquaintances have observed rainbow haloes around the summit, caused (if you are inclined to scientific explanations) by thin mist around the rocks and sunlight above, projecting shadows and catching and scattering the colours of the spectrum on water droplets. TC Lethbridge called this "the broken spectre", and Welbourne Tekh experienced it in a stunning form in 1997 when he climbed to the summit in clearing cloud, after heavy rain. I have been on the summit myself, on many occasions, when sea mist has been rolling in from the coast and the topmost crags stand like little islands above the surface of an ocean of white foam. Swirls of mist roll in slow motion through the gaps between the rocks, and the effect is eerie and very beautiful. I have described some of my own "cloud effect" experiences in the pages of the novels, and have given to Mistress Martha my own sense of surprise and wonderment. And many times every year, when high-altitude cirrus clouds are seen above the summit of the mountain, it is easy to see in them the shapes of angels' wings. On many such occasions I have heard the comment "Ah, the angels are flying over Carningli today."

Now, from the sublime to the ridiculous. At the top of the green track that leads up the mountain from the Dolrannog Road parking area, there are two masonry pillars with a narrow gap between them. One of my friends refers to these pillars as "the gateway to Carningli" and she will not go up the mountain, or come down off it, without passing between them. Above the gateway is the craggy mountain with all its mysteries, and below it is the humdrum world of everyday life. Fair enough, but the origins of the pillars are far more prosaic.

From what I can gather from the older local residents, the pillars are the most obvious relics of Carningli's industrial revolution. They are located at the top of the "Carningli Mountain Railway" which operated for a few years between the two World Wars during a time of substantial road improvements by Pembrokeshire County Council. The hundreds of little roads around Newport and Cilgwyn were being improved and provided with asphalt surfaces, and there was a great demand for crushed

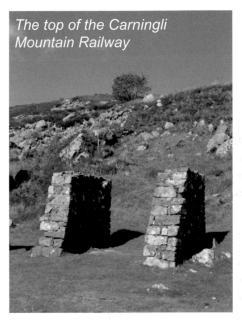

The top of the Carningli Mountain Railway

roadstone. Seeing a commercial opportunity in this, five Newport men decided that Carningli bluestone would fit the bill perfectly, since it could be obtained in good quantities from the lower scree slopes of the mountain with relatively little effort. They cleared things with the Commoners, applied to the Barony of Cemais for permission to take stone from the mountain (in exchange for a royalty for every ton taken), and did a deal with PCC.

They set up in business, and built a narrow-guage railway track about 500 yards long from the Cilgwyn Road up onto the mountain side. It runs almost east-west. In some places the men had to build embankments, and in others they had to excavate cuttings. They built a small crushing plant at the roadside, operated by a diesel engine. At the top of the incline they constructed two masonry pillars to support a large cable drum, the mountings for which were fixed on two large iron bolts on the top of each pillar. Another diesel engine was installed adjacent to the pillars, and this provided the power to rotate the drum and pull in the cable. They installed the railway track and bought three little railway trucks, which were connected together and then coupled to one end of the cable. When the trucks were stationed at the top of the incline they could be filled with blocks of stone carried from the quarrying area in a horse-drawn cart. Then they would be let down under the force of gravity, using a braking system on the cable drum to control the rate of descent. When they reached the bottom, they would be unloaded and the stone fed into the crushing plant. Then the upper diesel motor would be started, and the cable would be wound in again, pulling the three trucks back up to the top of the incline for a fresh load of stone.

I have never seen any written records (or photographs) of this short-lived industrial enterprise, but according to rumour it only lasted for a few years. Two men worked in the crushing plant and three up on the mountain. The "quarry" was maybe a hundred yards long, extending southwards along the contour from the winding gear. There are several obvious cuts into the mountain slope, but probably most of the rock which has been taken consisted of loose boulders and scree rather than solid rock. In the quarry the rock was broken up into stones about the size of footballs. Today we can still see still some piles of excavated stones here and there, but the most obvious trace of the quarrying activity is a cutting or gully which was used by the horse and cart for its journeys back and forth in delivering stone to the "loading bay".

Today all that can be seen of this little enterprise is the smooth green track of the incline, with a few metal sleepers showing through the turf, the winding-gear pillars, the overgrown quarrying area, and a little ruined hut to the north of the incline which might have been used as a shelter for the workmen. There is no trace at all of the crushing plant on the Cilgwyn Road.

And what was it that brought the Industrial Revolution on Carningli to an end? It must have been a truly spectacular event. According to legend, one day around 1933 the man in the quarry who had charge of the dynamite became a little too enthusiastic, and this led to an almighty explosion which caused fragments of shattered bluestone to rain down upon the roofs of all the cottages in the *cwm*. Thankfully nobody was hurt, but there was such an outcry that the firm's operating licence was revoked. The men dismantled their machinery and sold it off, leaving the mountain once again in the possession of sheep and angels.

Plas Ingli

Plas Ingli, the rebuilt house which is Martha's "House of Angels" in the stories, is a figment of my imagination. There never was a large gentry house in the position portrayed on the front cover of On Angel Mountain, and it appears to be there in the photograph because I have done a simple piece of "photo manipulation" using a software programme called PhotoDeluxe. I am sorry if I have caused offence in doing that!

But there was a little house about 300 yards to the south of my fantasy location, and on the map it is called Carningli Lodge. It is surrounded by a cluster of mature trees which is quite easy to spot from the Dolrannog Road car parking area. It lies on the edge of the common, only about 200 yards from the road. It is reached via a metal gate, and the tumbledown walls are just a few yards inside the boundary wall which separates the open land from the enclosed area which used to be cultivated. The house (if that is not too grand a word for it) was very small indeed, and I suspect that it was built around 1820 as a *ty unnos* (one-night house) following the end of the Napoleonic Wars, when land was scarce and there were too many mouths to feed. The cottage is not marked on the earliest detailed map I have, drawn by OS Surveyors in 1814. As described in several places in the novels, there was an old tradition in Wales that any landless person was entitled to build a house overnight on common land and to take possession of it thereafter as a freeholder. It was believed that this was enshrined in the Laws of Hywel Dda, but that was probably mere mythology. *Ty unnos* hovels were build around the fringes of the commons all over Wales, and in the Newport area several of them survive, especially on the north flank of Carningli along the edge of the bracken-covered common above Newport.

The ruins of Carningli Lodge. This is the back of the cottage, facing the mountain slope

To start with, Carningli Lodge was probably built overnight, in conditions of great secrecy, by the family and friends of the young couple who wanted to live there. The building materials would have been timber, daub and wattle, thatch and maybe even animal skins. If smoke was passing up the chimney or filtering through the thatch by dawn that was counted as a habitable dwelling, and the "residents" were also deemed to have the right to use as their curtilage all the land that could be reached by flinging an axe from the front door! Most of those who built hovels in this way were deemed to be illegal squatters; they were simply evicted and their nocturnal structures were demolished mercilessly by the landowners. But some survived, and those who put up their structures on land owned by the Barony of Cemais had a better chance of survival than most, because the Lord Marcher's place of residence (Newport Castle) was in ruins and he spent most of his time elsewhere.

For whatever reason, this little cottage DID survive, and over the years it was gradually extended and rebuilt in stone taken off the common. Today we can still see the pits from which stone was excavated. The cottage probably had a single chimney stack at one end and a roof of rough slates. There were probably only two small rooms, separated by a central passageway which ran from front door to back door. There may have been a sleeping loft above one of the rooms. There is an excavated passageway running southwards from the back door, and also a row of small structures, protected by a high hedge, that might have been used for the keeping of dogs, pigs, geese and hens. There were no other substantial buildings as far as we can see, and that means that there were no horses or cattle at Carningli Lodge. But there was a pleasant enclosed garden in front of the house, and another paddock to the south that might have been used for growing crops.

The land on which Carningli Lodge stands has for many years been owned by Gelli, and our farming neighbour Watkin Lewis was born in the cottage. It looks as if it was abandoned centuries ago, but it must have been habitable until the 1930's. Since then, the roof has fallen in or has been stripped away, and the walls have collapsed bit by bit until there is very little left. Some of the decent coin-stones have also been taken away. Effectively, it has been used as a sort of "quarry", as described in the first chapter of *On Angel Mountain*. The locals tell me that there used to be another hovel on the Dolrannog Road, between the edge of the common and Dolrannog Isaf, which

WAS known as Plas Ingli. That grand title must have been used with more than a touch of irony, and there is virtually no trace of it left today -- but on the 1814 map there is a little speck which shows where it was.

Now the old ruin is a very romantic and picturesque spot. I have always been drawn to it, for it is the place where I always hear the first cuckoo in spring, and where the wind always seems to be whispering through the gnarled and battered branches of the ancient ash trees. It is the first haven you come to if you are retreating down from the mountain in a sudden squall, or if you have walked from Bedd Morris in a howling gale. But is it more than just a pretty place? Let me tell you something else that might be considered strange and even spooky. When I was well into the writing of the Saga two female friends of mine related that when they had been working on a foundation art course at Trinity College Carmarthen as mature students, they had been set the task of making an artistic representation of somewhere that had a strong "female energy". Intuitively and independently they had both homed in on Carningli Lodge for their drawings and paintings, on the basis that they felt a strong female presence there..........

So what is my mental picture of Plas Ingli in its heyday? On the cover of the Greencroft Books edition of *On Angel Mountain*, and on page 22 of *House of Angels*, I give a representation of the house shortly after its rebuilding. Later, in my imagination, the buildings around the farmyard (to the left of the house) would have been repaired and brought back into full use, with the dairy and water tank closest to the house, and then the cowshed and stables on the north side, and the high-roofed barn on the south side. In the south-western (lower) corner of the yard there was an open area used for heaps of cow and horse manure which would be taken morning and evening in wheelbarrow loads from the cowshed and stable; these heaps grew day by day, and were whittled away during the winter muck-spreading season. The yard was paved not with cobbles but with large and irregular slate slabs bought cheaply from one of the local quarries. At the western end of the farmyard there would have been a coach-house and smaller buildings for dogs, pigs, chickens and geese, and beyond those there was the rickyard, located there because of the dictates of the terrain. In the southern and northern walls of the barn there were massive doors, capable of taking fully loaded horse-drawn wagons. The barley harvest would be brought in from the harvest fields through the southern door, and fodder, grain and chaff would be carried out through the northern door into the yard. When threshing and winnowing was going on, both of these huge doors would be open, so that the wind could blow through.

On the south side of the complex of buildings, there were two walled gardens. The smaller one, close to the house and barn, was Martha's "private garden" which she cultivated herself and which contained some fruit trees and some flower borders. The larger garden, located to the south of the rickyard, was dedicated to the growing of a large variety of vegetables, with fruit trees and soft fruit bushes close to the walls.

Animals, sledges and wheeled traffic would have moved about on several walled trackways, and there would have been many gates in and around the farm complex. The main driveway would have approached the front door of the house, but a little way down the drive there would have been a branch which looped round through the rickyard and into the farmyard. So farm traffic would not have passed in front of the main entrance. The door which was used almost all of the time, and which would normally have been left open, was the back door (on the gable end of the house), protected from the south-westerlies by an old scullery, and providing easy access to the dairy and the farmyard. A good model for my imaginary Plas Ingli can be visited today at Llannerchaeron, a National Trust property not far from Aberaeron and of exactly the right age -- but that was considerably more elaborate than the Plas, with a wonderful service block added onto the side of the John Nash mansion itself, and a physical separation of the house and the farm. Everything at Plas Ingli would have been cheek by jowl, for this was a very exposed location and shelter was everything.

The final feature which the reader of the novels needs to know about was the water pipe which carried the sacred water from Ffynnon Brynach down the slope and into the water tank adjacent to the dairy wall. This water was fresh and clean, and flowing all the time. The overflow from the tank passed in an underground culvert across the farmyard into a shallow pool near the barn (whence water could be taken for the animals), and thence to the duckpond near the walled garden and the rickyard. So there was no abundant water supply anywhere near the barn -- and this is important for the episode described on page 201 of *On Angel Mountain.*

Cilgwyn

Cilgwyn, nestling in a broad amphitheatre at the eastern end of Cwm Gwaun, is a locality and a community rather than a clustered settlement. It is best described as a "scattered hamlet", with only one real cluster of houses around Cilgwyn Bridge and with maybe fifty or sixty dwelling-houses in the bad old days. The main physical feature is the valley of the Afon Clydach, which joins the Afon Nyfer close to Llwyngwair. There is abundant woodland along the river, but the most extensive woodlands are in the east, where Pentre Ifan and Tycanol Woods clothe the rocky slopes beyond the spur of Carnedd Meibion Owen. There are tors in the woods, but the most prominent ones are on the skyline above the top edge of the wood -- four splendid rocky prominences which are reputed to be the petrified remains of the last four giants to have inhabited these parts. To the west the *cwm* is protected by the mass of Carningli.

The dwellings were sprinkled more or less at random across the face of the land, some on sandy and gravelly hummocks and others on areas of thin acid soil. The majority housed labourers or peasants, some of whom had a garden or a small paddock to help them to eke out a living. Some larger houses were used by the tenant farmers and their families, and there were three or four more substantial buildings put up by those who owned land and who counted themselves as minor gentry. There was a church and a Baptist Chapel, and a number of skilled craftsmen including a blacksmith, a miller and a farrier.

Although the community was tied quite closely to Newport it was not far from self-sufficiency, and many crafts including weaving, knitting, carpentry, candle-making, wood-turning, basketry and leatherworking were practised by people who could turn their hands to almost anything. Money was in short supply, and bartering was commonplace. Cilgwyn split its loyalties between Newport on the coast, Pontfaen in the Gwaun Valley, and Brynberian to the south-east. The road from New England to Dolrannog and Penrhiw did not exist in 1814, and it was probably

The porch of the ruinous Cilgwyn Church

easier for the farming community on the southern slope of Carningli to get to Llannerch and Pontfaen than to travel to Newport.

After the middle of the nineteenth century, the rise of the merchant class brought newcomers into the *cwm*, and many of the old houses changed hands. With more cash in circulation and with great improvements in the road network, Newport became more important as a shopping centre and the locals did less and less business with Pontfaen and Brynberian. Well within living memory there was a post office and two pubs in Cilgwyn, and the mill continued to operate until 1948. But after the Second World War there was not enough business for these little businesses to continue, and the community changed again. The place kept its strong sense of community and "separateness", but as young people left the land and moved away, more and more families who spoke no Welsh began to purchase properties as they came on the market, and the Welshness of Cilgwyn was certainly diluted. In the 1970's and 1980's Cilgwyn became one of the great centres of the British "self-sufficiency" movement, with key figures like John and Sally Seymour at Fachongle Isaf and Satish Kumar and June Mitchell at Pentre Ifan preaching the virtues of simplicity and self-reliance to a worldwide audience. John Seymour was particularly influential, and his best-selling books attracted many others to the *cwm*. Even today Fachongle and Brithdir Mawr are famous for their residents who do things differently and who dare to challenge the planning rules. Mistress Martha would have been proud of them!

Newport

Newport is an ancient borough which was for many centuries (until it was overtaken by Fishguard) the main town on the North Pembrokeshire coast. Trefdraeth, its Welsh name, means "the town by the beach", and it derives from the proximity of the vast sandy sweep of Traeth Mawr on the Nevern estuary. The original settlement site may well have been downslope of the present town, on the southern shore of the estuary where there is a strange earthwork referred to as Yr Hen Gastell or The Old Castle. In pre-Norman times, when the Vikings were roving up and down the west coast of Wales, there was probably just a scattered community here, made up of farmers, fishermen and merchants. Some of them would have lived at the mouth of the river, in the place we now call Parrog.

The arrival of the Normans led to several centuries of social upheaval, with motte and bailey and stone castles being built across North Pembrokeshire by both the Welsh princes and the invaders during the ebbs and flows of their military campaigns and political alliances. The main invisible product of this time was the Barony of

Newport Castle. The ruins were converted into a comfortable residence in the mid-nineteenth century

Cemais, which -- against all the odds -- survives to this day. The Lord Marcher (when he was in residence) controlled his vast estates from a fine stone castle built on a spur, very close to the new town centre. It was built around 1200, with a fine Anglo-Norman church in its shadow. The building of stone trading quays on the south side of the Nevern estuary, and the first use of the name "Newport", came in the early Middle Ages. Parrog, which was really the new port, expanded as the home of a small seafaring community. A short distance inland, the Norman town grew apace under the protection of the castle battlements, with streets running downslope towards the shore and with more than 200 burgage plots occupied by burgesses or freemen. There were at least three water mills within the town boundaries, many craft establishments and traders, and more than a fair share of inns. Schools and chapels came later, built during the social and evangelical transformations of the eighteenth and nineteenth centuries. Later still merchants, craftsmen, shopkeepers, doctors and bankers, teachers and "lodging-house proprietors" all helped to change the face of the town.

As an ancient borough Newport has a number of very old buildings, and the medieval pattern of small streets has survived intact. Today the town's axis runs east - west, along the A487 road. The castle and St Mary's church still look down on the town. Other interesting buildings include the Sessions House, the nonconformist chapels, the Castle Hotel, the shop fronts on Market Street, the assemblage of old cottages and guest houses on the Parrog sea front, and a number of fine old houses on the outskirts of the town, some of which were built by ancient mariners who risked life and limb to make their fortunes. There are few town centre buildings of outstanding quality, but some are listed, and the small-scale and varied styles of house fronts, cottages and commercial premises gives Newport a charming and unpretentious character. Houses and shop fronts co-exist side by side in a happy jumble. In recent years many property owners in the town centre have renovated buildings attrac-

Carreg Coetan Arthur, a cromlech within the town boundary

tively, restoring stone facing, slate roofing and other vernacular features. Window boxes and hanging baskets add bright splashes of colour during the summer months.

One of the most important "ancient monuments" within the confines of the town is the *cromlech* (Neolithic burial chamber) of Carreg Coetan Arthur, a short distance south of Pen-y-bont and standing incongruously in a small housing estate. On the outskirts of the town there are other ancient features which inform us about aspects of local life in days gone by. These include the *cromlechs* of Cerrig y Gof, Llechydrybedd and Trellyffaint, the Iron Age hillforts at Carningli and Carnffoi, Bronze Age settlement features on Mynydd Caregog, the old "sea quarries" on the cliffs west of Cat Rock, and the old Pont Ceunant viaduct. Closer to town are the Shiphill limekiln (in Nevern parish), the magnificent old cattle pound off Ffordd Bedd Morris, and the Iron Bridge and medieval stepping stones across the estuary between Newport and Berry Hill. Some of these features are visited by Martha and mentioned in the pages of the Saga.

The old lime-kiln at Shiphill

One of the old sea quarries. This one is at Hescwm

In some ways the coastline of the Newport area is its most valuable asset. The Normans made Newport the headquarters of the Barony of Cemais because it was accessible from the sea and because of its sheltered estuary. Many hundreds of years later it was because of the beauty of the Nevern Estuary, Newport Bay and its high cliffs, that the area was included in the Pembrokeshire Coast National Park when it was designated in 1952. Particularly attractive features of the coastal environment are Traeth Mawr and the estuary inland as far as the Iron Bridge, the sand dune areas, and the high cliffs of Pen Morfa. In Martha's day the coast would have been very different. For a start, the sea quarries were operating noisily on several sections of the cliffline. There was of course no coastal footpath, and bird life would have been much more abundant than today. Martha loved the coast, but it was not frequently visited by those in search of beauty and tranquillity; and that suited Martha and Owain very well when they were desperate for another passionate picnic.

In the modern Newport a number of old traditions still survive, possibly because (like Laugharne on the coast of Carmarthen Bay) there is great social stability here and a small enough population to ensure that supermarket chains have not been tempted to move in! With some very ancient families, a fascinating social structure, a multitude of clubs and committees, a singular lack of respect for authority and a reputation for rugged individuality if not ill-discipline, the modern town is a wonderful and eccentric place. Among its assets are a splendid community spirit and a clean and beautiful environment. There is also a continuing respect for the old way of doing things. That can be very irritating for those who want change -- as Mistress Martha discovered long ago!

One of the oldest traditions in the community is the Beating of the Bounds, described in Chapter 9 of *House of Angels*. This involved the marking and inspection of the ancient borough boundary. The great standing stone of Bedd Morris, on the mountain between Newport and Pontfaen, is just one of the boundary markers between the parishes of Newport and Llanychlwydog. It bears the initials of Thomas Davies Lloyd, who was Lord of Cemais in the mid-1800s and who was responsible for the conversion of part of the ruined Newport Castle into a Victorian mansion. The stone is on the route of the annual perambulation by aldermen, burgesses, townspeople and visitors, which takes place in August each year. In the old days the *crachach* travelled on horseback, while the parishioners and children followed on foot. The ceremony, which may well be several centuries old, was designed originally to check the parish boundaries and to ensure that there was no encroachment upon them. The bounds were beaten regularly (every seven years) between 1777 and 1888, but then the custom lapsed to be revived in 1964 by Dillwyn Miles who was then Mayor. Nowadays the riders and walkers of this soft generation do not have the energy to follow the whole of the boundary around the parish. But Bedd Morris is a key location on the shortened route because it is here that small boys are beaten (very gently indeed) so that they will remember exactly where the boundary runs.

There are some very old institutions in Newport, and among these the most important are the Court Leet and the Court Baron. Both have been involved in the administration of law and order in Newport and the Barony of Cemais for about 800 years. Broadly, the Court Leet was made up of local burgesses and freeholders who were originally responsible, through a "grand inquisition of jurors", for dealing with petty crime, collecting tolls and rents, looking after highways, and protecting the rights of rich and poor. The grand jury also submitted a list of three burgesses each year to the Lord of Cemais, so that he could choose one to be Mayor of the Town. The chosen mayor was sworn in at the November Court, and thereafter through the year he would be responsible for the day-to-day administration of the town with the help of a bailiff and pound-keeper and four petty constables.

The Court Baron or Hundred Court dealt with matters relating to customs and tenancy agreements, trespass, slander, debts and land management matters in the Newport part of the Barony. It was held every other Monday, and down through the centuries it clearly had a lot of work to do! The old records show that many of the cases dealt with by the court involved disputes which would come under the Civil Law rather than the Criminal Law today; but through the centuries there have been many celebrated and exciting cases. No less important was the quiet work of the Court in determining grazing levels on the common lands of the parish, looking after rights of turbary (peat-cutting), piscary (fishing), the collection of firewood and building stone, and sorting out the ownership of stray animals including sheep, cattle, ponies and goats.

It is a testament to the determination of generations of mayors, aldermen and burgesses in Newport that the ancient institutions mentioned above are still going strong. Somehow or other, they have survived Nineteenth and Twentieth Century Acts of Parliament and other legislative measures designed to reform local government. Sometimes Newport argued successfully for special exemptions, and sometimes (according to legend) Newport was simply forgotten about by the law-makers of Westminster! But somehow, by a combi-

96

nation of luck and good judgement, Newport is still designated an Ancient Borough. Its mayor is still appointed in November by the Lady Marcher, who receives from the new incumbent a red rose as a sign of allegiance. (The Lord Mayor of London is the only other civic head appointed in November.) The Court Leet and Court Baron still meet in May and September, and appoint new burgesses. A third court is held to coincide with the appointment of the Mayor. And since 1964 a special annual court has been held towards the end of August to coincide with the Beating of the Bounds. This latter court is the only one which is open to the public.

There must have been a Town Crier in Newport since the Middle Ages, but records are sadly lacking. It is known that at least two of the town criers in recent decades were members of the Varney family. After a lapse of about 30 years a new Town Crier was appointed following a competition organised by the Chamber of Trade and the Court Leet in 1988. A special uniform in red, white and black (the colours of the Ancient Borough's coat of arms) was designed and made, and this is now worn by the incumbent on those occasions when official announcements are required in the town. The Town Crier normally rings his bell and "cries" (reading from his special scroll) in the town centre, but in the past he has been called in to officiate at *Cnapan* games, carnivals and so forth at other local venues.

Newport's traditional annual fair is dedicated to St Curig, an Irish saint who lived in the 8th-9th Centuries and who had some links with St Patrick. Nobody is quite sure what contact he may have had with Newport, but there was a Capel Curig near Newport Bridge, with a sacred well (Ffynnon Gurig) nearby. Possibly the parish church in the upper part of the town was also dedicated to St Curig before the Normans arrived. The feast day of St Curig was originally 16 June, but when the Gregorian Calendar was adopted in 1752 the date was changed to 27 June. Ever since the Middle Ages the great fair was a holiday for local people, an occasion for merrymaking, buying and selling, and an occasion for the Mayor to raise revenue through the collection of tolls on livestock sales and from stallholders. There was much hiring of farm servants, settling of debts, and financial wheeling and dealing between farmers and merchants. The fair sometimes lasted for several days, and the Mayor required the attendance of all burgesses and the help of up to a dozen hired hands to control unruly animals and inebriated citizens.

In the 1700's and 1800's the fair went through a number of phases of decline and resurgence, related partly to changes in the farming economy and partly to problems concerning the tolls levied by the Mayor on behalf of the Lord of the Barony. Neither the local burgesses nor the horse and cattle dealers who came to the town were happy about the tolls, and the old records are full of petitions and disputes concerning toll avoidance. In 1843 there was a move to start a rival toll-free fair in Maenclochog, and another in Eglwyswrw in 1851. There was even an illegal fair in Newport in 1862, and eventually the tolls were dropped. As recently as 1935 the fair was a very large affair, with hundreds of horses, cattle and pigs lined up along West Street and preventing vehicular traffic from passing through the town. Market Street was lined with stalls selling fruit and vegetables, clothes and fabrics and a vast range of cheap-jack items for town-house and farm. There were games and amusements of all sorts. Sometimes the fair was so big that stalls extended down Long Street as well. There were even roundabouts and stalls in a travelling fun-fair that took place in a field adjacent to Llysmeddyg.

Ffair Gurig faded away during the Second World War, but was revived in 1951 by Dillwyn Miles during his first term as Mayor. Nowadays it brings Ffair Gurig Week to a climax as a modest but jolly occasion on which local organisations and traders set up stalls on Long Street to raise funds for assorted good causes.

In the stories Martha has a love-hate relationship with Newport. On the one hand she thinks it is smelly and dirty and too "urban" to be trusted, but she has many friends in town and she enjoys visiting them. She also enjoys being admired when she is out on the street, dressed in her finery. She quite enjoys it when her antics cause tongues to wag, and she never forgets that when she is whipped through the streets in *On Angel Mountain* the townspeople sustain her in her shame and her agony, and give her the strength to face down her tormentors. She also grows very close to the poor people of the town during the "dysentery sickness" and becomes something of a local heroine in the process. In fact she always feels closer to those who live in poverty than to those who live in wealthy ostentation, and throughout her life she exists in a state of conflict with those who see themselves as the leaders of the town. Her natural allies are Skiff Abraham and his cronies, and she is never happier than when her spies from among the riff-raff are hard at work, keeping her informed of the murky goings-on in taverns and on dark street corners. She exploits them certainly, for she knows that they are all a little in love with her, but she also defends them when they need defending, and she knows that when she needs them they will turn out in force, without a moment's hesitation. So they are angels too, maybe not as white as those in Heaven or as black as those on Carningli, but an interesting shade of grey.

Parrog

As indicated above, Parrog has been used as a port for well over a thousand years, and the people of the little community have always looked on themselves as somewhat "apart" from the people of Newport. Traditionally, this has been a place of sailors and sailing ships, and there is still a nautical feeling here, with salt in the air, people messing about in boats, and tall tales in the bar of the Boat Club.

The Parrog itself has been dramatically changed in appearance over the centuries. Originally "the port" probably consisted of nothing more than an open foreshore where small sailing ships were built and repaired, and where cargoes were loaded and unloaded. They came in on a high tide, were loaded and unloaded by a procession of horses and carts when the tide was low, and then sailed off again on another high tide. That was laborious, dirty and risky work, and ships were endangered if they were in the estuary and on the beach when the wind was in the north at half-tide. Ships which are half-

The Parrog, showing one of the lime-kilns in the foreground, with the lime-burner's cottage on the left

afloat can of course break their backs if afflicted by swells rolling over a submerged bar. In Norman times the estuary was not so heavily silted, and access would have been easier at half-tide than it is today. There might have been a stone quay and a slipway. As commercial activity and shipbuilding expanded in the Middle Ages, Parrog became one of the most important ports on Cardigan Bay, with exports of wool, rough woollen cloth, slates and salted herrings, and imports of coal, limestone, salt, wine, grain, tar, iron, soap, and a host of other necessities. The cottages on the sea front were built by fishermen, sailors and craftsmen involved in the local shipyards; and larger houses were built here and in the town by merchants and sea captains.

At last it became apparent that storehouses and proper quays were needed, but there were no major investments until the eighteenth century. Then four lime kilns were built on a spit of land projecting out from the shore, and between 1760 and the end of the century several storehouses and storage yards were built nearby. Part of the marsh was reclaimed. Work was started on quay walls and slip-ways, but the major work of defending the Parrog from the sea was not undertaken till 1816-25, when slates from the nearby sea quarries were brought in and used for the dry-stone walling which we can still see today. In its heyday the peninsular "port" at Parrog had two large storehouses and several smaller ones, a number of small cottages including one used by a lime-burner, and four lime kilns. One of the large storehouses was demolished in 1922 when the owner lost a wager, which resulted in it being dismantled so that the stone could be used in the building of the Memorial Hall! The other building was saved when it was bought by the Newport Boat Club, and subsequently converted and extended in several stages.

Parrog: the marsh. One of the old ship-yards was located on the shore

Ship-building was an important local activity, and there were two shipyards, one on the shore of the marsh on the eastern flank of the Parrog peninsula, and the other further up the estuary in the creek known as Bryncyn or Shiphill. Actually they were not proper shipyards at all, but simply level pieces of land just above high water mark from which launching could take place via a temporary slipway. Sometimes two or three vessels may have been under construction side by side on the shore, especially at the Parrog site. On average, a ship would take about six months to build. Only about a dozen ships were built at Newport in the eighteenth century, but after 1800 the rate of construction greatly increased, and well over 50 vessels were constructed over a period of 40 years. Mostly they were small sloops, brigs and schooners, generally less than 50 tons in weight and never more than 200 tons. The main shipbuilders were John Havard and his son Levi, but the shipbuilding work involved carpenters, sail-makers, blacksmiths, rope-makers and various other craftsmen, and the industry was of great importance to the local economy over a period of more than a century.

In the heyday of Newport sea-trading, around 1800-1850, over 100 sailing ships were based at the port, with many others calling regularly to pick up or deposit cargoes. Locally, the ownership of vessels was divided into 64 shares, and these shares were often owned by merchants, sea captains, and farmers. But the biggest shipowners of all were the members of the Davies family of Cardigan and Newport, who owned over 50 vessels as well as substantial property in Newport, Cardigan and St Dogmaels. Many male members of the family were mariners themselves, and several of them were lost at sea. In the Saga, Martha invests some of her money in trading vessels, and relishes the risks involved in big winnings and big losings.

The coming of the railway to Pembrokeshire around 1850 signalled the end of the sailing ship era, but because Newport was remote from the expanding railway network the port at Parrog continued in use until after the First World War. As late as 1880 there were over a hundred shipments a year being handled, but after that there was a sharp decline, and after 1888 steamships began to replace the little smacks, schooners and ketches. By this time, silting in the estuary was a severe problem, and it was only on the highest of tides that vessels were able to approach the Parrog quays for loading and unloading. Among the last ships trading to Newport were the *Mary Jane Lewis* and the famous ketch *Garlandstone,* and the last shipment was in 1934.

In the stories Martha is very fond of the Parrog, for a number of reasons. She enjoys the atmosphere of the place, populated as it is by fish-wives, lodging-house keepers, prostitutes, traders and sea-men. It is really no place for fine ladies, but she comes here anyway, over and again, especially after she has forged her firm friendship with Patty Ellis. It is here that Martha meets Eli Davids on his death-bed. It is here, in the mortuary on the quayside, that David's body is laid out following the fatal *Cnapan* Contest of 1805. And it is here (just around the corner into the estuary) that Alban Watkins meets his gruesome end. Strong characters, strong events, and salt in the air.

Tycanol Wood

This ancient patch of woodland, which is really an extension of the much larger Pentre Ifan Wood, is another of North Pembrokeshire's "magic places." It occupies a spur and a little pattern of small val-leys beneath the skyline tors of Carnedd Meibion Owen, and the land surface is clothed with twisted oaks and other deciduous trees and moss-covered boulders. In the spring there are great swathes of bluebells in bloom before the trees come into full leaf. There are li-chens everywhere (400 species recorded to date), and the special ecology of the wood is the main reason for its designation as a na-tional nature reserve. But the thing which gives Ty Canol its magical feel is the rock. There is hard volcanic rock everywhere -- underfoot, on rough rock faces adjacent to the footpath through the wood, in boulders and gravelly patches in the depressions, and especially in the tors. It is extremely rare to find upstanding crags and pinnacles of rock in the middle of an ancient oak woodland, but here they are, all over the place. After many visits to the woods over the years, I have still not discovered all of them, let alone explored them. Here and there stone walls, paddocks and abandoned trackways and meadows show us that past residents have practiced the arts and crafts of agriculture around the lower fringes of the woodland, and on a wide platform bounded by a cliff there is a small defended site with embankments, presumably dating from the Iron Age.

Part of the magical woodland of Tycanol

Towards the top edge of the wood, not far from the gate which leads up to Carnedd Meibion Owen, there is a little cave. It is not easy to find, but it is cosy and dry if not exactly comfortable. I have seen it referred to as Brynach's Cave, the Cave of the Dark Goddess, and the Druid's Cave. So for better or for worse, it is invested with symbolism -- and there is a long tradition that the "oak groves" of Ty Canol were associated with Druidic rites in the days when an Iron Age or Celtic community might have lived here. The cave does not seem particularly mystical to me, but perhaps it does have good vibes, and the one good story about the cave that I have come across relates to an army deserter or conscientious objector who lived in it during the Second World War and who was fed and otherwise looked after by friendly local people. According to legend, he was never discovered by the authorities, and then disappeared when the war came to an end. Again, Mistress Martha would have approved........

When I had my strange turn on Gran Canaria in 1999, I knew immediately that Coed Tycanol would be the place where Martha would make love with David when she was young and with Amos when she was old -- and that this would be the location for the final bloody and dramatic episode of the Saga in which Amos loses his life. So it would be a place replete with symbolism, and I have been reminded by a number of readers that in a sunlit glade among the Tycanol oaks three people -- Martha, David and Amos -- lose their virginity. This is where Martha conceives at least two of her babies in ecstasy, and this is where the sad and lonely figure of Mary Roberts commits suicide after betraying the man with whom she was obsessed. Finally this is where Amos sacrifices his own life to save Martha. Passion, seduction, betrayal, self-sacrifice and murder all one one small patch of grass surrounded by trees. If you want to see a Druidic connection in all of that, who am I to argue?

An old drawing of a Druid carrying a stave and a twig of oak leaves. Did the Druids use Tycanol Wood in their ceremonies? It's quite possible..........

105

Cwm Gwaun

During the Ice Age, Pembrokeshire was inundated on at least two occasions by the ice of the Irish Sea Glacier. The ice did not come down from the mountains, but in from where the sea had been, flowing from NW to SE. During the earlier of these two glaciations the glacier probably extended as far east as Wiltshire and as far south as the Scilly Isles. The ice over this part of Pembrokeshire was probably at least 2,000 feet thick. At the end of this glaciation, about 100,000 years ago, vast quantities of meltwater were produced; and in the area around Fishguard, Trecwn and the Gwaun Valley this meltwater eroded a spectacular series of deep steep-sided channels.

Cwm Gwaun

These are called "subglacial meltwater channels", because the meltwater which eroded them was flowing under great pressure far beneath the downwasting ice surface. Under these conditions certain sections of the channels were cut by meltwater actually flowing uphill, as it does in a pipe when there is adequate pressure. So all of the valleys have "humps" in their floors. The valleys are also peculiar in that they are "through valleys" with no heads and with very low gradients; in places it is difficult to work out the direction of water flow at the time when they were carved out of the landscape.

Cwm Gwaun is about 10 km long and in places more than 100m deep, opening in the west into the amphitheatre of Cilgwyn, and in the east into Fishguard Bay in the harbour of lower Town. It is the best-known and most-photographed of all the channels, and landscape scientists reckon that it is the best example of a subglacial meltwater channel anywhere in the world. That is why it is classified as a nature reserve, and why it appears in many geology and geomorphology text-books. But it is also famous because it is so serenely beautiful, and because segments of the ancient Welsh wildwood have managed to survive here whereas in most other parts of West Wales they have been cut down and replaced by farmland or by more modern woodlands. Even where the woodlands are only a century or two old, they are dominated by flimsy and twisted sessile oak trees which create a very special ecological niche for other plants and animals. The woodlands are particularly rich in lichens, and the sheer diversity of these strange and primitive plants can be seen best in the little valleys which run down the sides of the main channel, in habitats dominated by waterfalls cascading torrents and deep rock pools. Pandy, not far from Gelli Fawr and Llannerch, is one such place where the abundant water was used in a little fulling mill. I used one of the pools as the location for the scene in *House of Angels* where Martha spies on Owain as he innocently floats about in the water, as naked as the day he was born.

Cowslips in Cwm Gwaun

The valley community is undoubtedly a strong one, even though there are only two small hamlets (Pontfaen and Llanychaer) between Cilgwyn and Fishguard, and relatively few farms and cottages. There are two small churches, one chapel, one inn and one public house. The only school now left in the valley (near Pontfaen) hangs on to life in the face of falling pupil rolls and primary school closures all over North Pembrokeshire. Probably the population is more or less the same today as it was in 1800. The language which is in most common use in the *cwm* is Welsh, and many families have occupied the same farms and cottages for generation after generation. This means that there is a social stability in the valley which is virtually unknown anywhere else in West Wales, and the community is famous in particular for the manner in which *Hen Galan* (The Old New Year) is still celebrated on 13th January, providing another opportunity for conviviality almost a fortnight after the New New Year. The festivities are described in various places in the Saga, and I have imagined that the Morgan family of Plas Ingli always celebrated *Hen Galan* with the Laugharnes of Pontfaen. Nowadays the celebrations are not exactly private, but the local families are wary of outsiders who try to muscle in on their parties and especially of BBC men like the late Fife Robertson who turned up with a film crew and reported on proceedings in a manner that was deemed to be condescending!

It is strange, to my way of thinking, that a valley as beautiful and serene as Cwm Gwaun should have a reputation for being somewhat spooky and forbidding. I have known for many years that there are fascinating stories of ghosts, phantom funerals, corpse candles and other supernatural phenomena associated with death in the valley, but it was not until I set about systematically collecting Pembrokeshire folk tales in the years 1990-1996 that the sheer abundance of these stories was confirmed. Maybe this somewhat ghoulish reputation has something to do with the medieval *Life of St Brynach* which relates that the area's favourite saint tried to establish his monastic community in Cwm Gwaun, only to be driven away by ghostly wailings and horrible howlings. He concluded rather quickly that the local spirits were not at all friendly. So he moved on to Nevern, where he did find peace and quiet.

Cwm Gwaun figures very prominently in the life history of Mistress Martha, with villains living at Llannerch, Gelli Fawr and Llanychaer, and with the beloved Owain living first at Pontfaen and later (following the demise of Alban Watkins) at Llannerch. Martha walks into the valley along the Penrhiw - Llannerch track on many occasions, and the woodlands provide the setting for much of her affair with Owain. In the later novels the focus moves to Llanychaer, and the old house occupied (in my imagination) by old Squire Price and his tragic son Iestyn, and then later by Brynach and his children.

5. Mistress Martha

When a character as exotic, beautiful and passionate as Martha Morgan walks into one's life in the middle of the night, when one is at a low ebb, one cannot fail to be impressed! I suppose I fell in love with her there and then, and have remained in love ever since. (My wife Inger doesn't seem to mind too much, since she and Martha might just be closely related!) An author MUST love his heroes or heroines if he is to inject passion and realism into his narrative and his portrayals of character. I love some of the others too -- especially Joseph Harries, Bessie Walter, Owain Laugharne, Patty Ellis and Amos Jones. Perversely, I am also quite fond of some of my villains, including Moses Lloyd, George Price and Alban Watkins. Nobody is all bad or all good, and I have tried to show that some of the villains who prowl through the pages of the Saga are also victims, pushed into the pathways of evil by force of circumstance. Even Martha, the matriarch of Plas Ingli, is anything but perfect.

Virtues and Vices

At the beginning of *On Angel Mountain* Martha is pregnant, confused and suicidal. She is suffering from morning sickness, and she has just been forced into a hasty marriage by a family obsessed with status and reputation. She loves her new husband David, but so low is her own self-esteem that she thinks he will be happier without her. From that low point she gradually struggles uphill to achieve some sort of equilibrium, and with the support of her new family (and new friends like the Wizard of Werndew) she discovers that she is loved and appreciated by others. As the very young mistress of a struggling estate she starts to assert herself -- then she loses her baby and plunges into a black and very prolonged depression. Is she a manic depressive? Probably not -- but then I'm not a psychiatrist! She certainly wallows in her misery, on that occasion and on a number of others later in the stories, but she does have a capacity for switching from misery to elation quite rapidly -- and as she grows older, she learns how to banish her demons. And she is anything but a self-obsessed introvert.

She has many virtues, as befits a heroine. She is more liberal, more tolerant and more free-thinking than she has any right to be, and in that sense she lives "outside her period in history." But that's how she came to me, and I had to be true to the picture of her which I held in my mind's eye ever since that strange night of delirium on Gran Canaria. Over and again I pondered whether I was creating "a modern woman in fancy dress", but repeatedly I decided that every heroine worth her salt has to stand out from the crowd, and has to be more beautiful, more passionate, more impetuous, more intelligent than all of the other women who wander in and out of the stories. Think of Lizzie Bennett in *Pride and Prejudice*, or Moll Flanders, or Jane Eyre, or Portia and Ophelia in the works of Shakespeare! If they were not "over the top" in some way, would we remember them?

One of Martha's characteristics is her unpretentiousness. Most of the members of her class kept their distance from labourers, servants and tenants in the early nineteenth century, and worked hard at maintaining their status and protecting privilege and power. In the stories, Martha hates all of that, and is drawn instinctively to the underprivileged. She identifies far more closely with Patty the prostitute than she does with Mistress Maria Rice, and not just because the latter is mean-spirited and arrogant. Her biggest friends, as she goes through life, are Ellie Bowen and Mary Jane Laugharne, who share her instinct for philanthropy and her dislike for pretension. And then, in *Flying with Angels*, when the large and earthy Mistress Delilah Gwynne bursts upon the scene, she can hardly contain her delight at the discovery of a kindred spirit. Martha's close identification with the poor is forced upon her to some degree by the circumstances in which the Morgan family finds itself -- effectively bankrupt, and brought low by the inferno which destroyed all the estate buildings and which killed five members of the family. But there was no gaping gulf between the gentry and the "lower classes" in Wales, partly because most of the gentry were less affluent than their counterparts in England and partly because there was much less cash in circulation. The estates were smaller and very vulnerable. "In kind" payments were common, and there was a complex system of debt recording and debt adjustment among members of the same class and among different classes too. Meals were shared, and work was shared. Very strong friendships were forged between the masters and mistresses of the smaller estates and their servants, tenants and labourers -- and the sort of social divide that we become aware of in *Pride and Prejudice* existed only on the biggest estates. In her relationships with those who might be below her socially, Martha is picking up on the easy familiarity which already exists in the relationships between Grandma Jane and Mrs Owen or between David and Billy. But she takes that familiarity and mutual respect to a new level, and makes bonds that are so tight as to make Plas Ingli a unique and wonderful place. If the house is inhabited by angels, then Martha clearly has more than a little to do with it.

So for better or for worse, Martha is a nineteenth-century version of super-woman. From the beginning she is very beautiful and very sexy, and as she blossoms into womanhood she gains a reputation as the most beautiful woman in Wales. Little wonder that many readers have said that Catherine Zeta Jones has to play her when the film comes to be made! She is well educated, and has a very enquiring mind. She is a competent musician and a moderately talented artist. She speaks English, Welsh, French and Dimetian Welsh fluently. She reads widely, and is attracted to "subversive" or radical literature. Her liberal views frequently lead her into trouble, and it is quite natural that she should be concerned about the plight of slaves and convicts and all those who might be oppressed or victimized by the crown, the government, and impersonal institutions. She has concerns about voting reform and womens' rights, and she sympathises with the Chartists -- at least until they start to split apart and lose control of extremist elements. She is immediately drawn to the

Rebecca Rioters since she understands what their grievances are and sees (better than most of her peers) what happens to families struggling against poverty and disease. She is not particularly religious, but goes through the motions of being a worthy member of the established church and goes through life trying to be a "better person." She flirts with Methodism for a while, and finds the devotion and kindness of the Non-conformists appealing. But at the same time she is irritated by their evangelical zeal and their unshakeable conviction that they are saved while others are condemned to hellfire and damnation. She is, as she admits now and then in the pages of her diaries, not averse to a little jolly sin now and then. She is also perfectly happy to shelter criminals, to drink smuggled gin, to tell lies, and to withhold her tithe payments in protest against the arrogance and insensitivity of the Church.

Martha's water-colour painting of the Plas shortly after the completion of rebuilding work

Mistress Martha

But Martha has a host of virtues too. She is brave, loyal to her husband and her family, and fiercely protective of those in her care once she is widowed and responsible for the safety of the Plas Ingli estate. She has enormous generosity of spirit, and makes spontaneous gestures of support when others might back off. Think about the welcome she gives to Patty the prostitute, or to Will the petty criminal, or to Zeke Tomos, who goes on to betray her. She often acts impulsively and on the basis of intuition and instinct. She makes huge self-sacrifices for the good of others. She puts herself in danger over and again, often because she is seeking to help those who do not necessarily deserve her assistance or her loyalty. For example, she plunges into the task of helping the sick and the dying during the cholera epidemic of 1797 without any thought for her own wellbeing. She goes to Ireland to help the starving during the Irish Potato Famine, and becomes seriously ill in the process. She sees beauty all around her, and takes an almost child-like pleasure in simple things -- such as standing on the mountain-top in the wind with her hair streaming behind her and her arms stretched out wide. She loves her children and her grand-children, and welcomes back Daisy, the black sheep of the family, when she returns after years of loose living in London. She fights to keep her family together when stresses and strains occur because of grief, or bankruptcy or other disasters. On those occasions she is a diplomat as well as a matriarch. In some ways she is also naive, and has a tendency to think well of others when suspicion might be more appropriate. But she trusts her family and her servants to look after her when she makes misjudgments, and indeed they do just that. She is a prudent and wise estate manager, and she knows how to inspire loyalty, give responsibility to others, and reward enterprise. She never stops learning, and wants others to learn and to better themselves -- to the extent that she becomes a great benefactor of the Circulating Schools. She is generous to a fault, and one of the ironies of the Saga is that having protected her precious treasure and left it in the ground as a "family insurance" for more than fifty years, she finally digs it up and gives most of it away.

113

As mentioned in Chapter 3, the thing that I love most about Martha is her sheer bloody-mindedness and her determination that she **will not be overwhelmed** by grief or misfortune, or even betrayal, and that she will bounce up again with a smile on her face whenever she is knocked down. That resilience is the characteristic that I admire most in other people. Martha is no victim and no stoic. And she is not exactly serene or gentle either. She is too much of a fighter to aspire to sainthood -- but maybe she does have some of the virtues of an angel. When readers say to me "Poor Martha! What a miserable life she has!" I have to remind them that she actually has quite a lot of fun. She has an active sex life well into old age, and enjoys the love and loyalty of all the "angels" who look after her. She makes opportunities for herself to do all sorts of exciting things, including riding out with the Rebecca Rioters when she is in her mid-sixties! And she never ceases to take pleasure in striding out over the common, climbing among the crags on her sacred mountain, lying on her back in the middle of a flower meadow on a June day, or watching butterflies and lizards with her children and then her grandchildren. She has jovial and influential friends too, and a busy social life surrounded by admirers. And more often than I care to mention, she seems to enjoy the freedom of being a "merry widow." How many times, one wonders, was the episode on the last page of *Rebecca and the Angels* repeated, maybe in the company of other gentlemen?

And so to Martha's vices. There are plenty of these. Her wild swings of mood make her difficult to live with, and her impulsive and erratic actions sometimes bring family and friends to the edge of despair. She does become very self-obsessed at times, and has to be reminded quite forcefully (by Grandma Jane, Bessie and Mrs Owen) that she should think more of the impacts of her actions on those who love her. She weeps a lot for the sins of the world and for the suffering of others -- but maybe that is a virtue rather than a vice. She is economical with the truth when it suits her, and she is sometimes quite devious in her behaviour. She learns how to "use the system" and does it frequently. In *House of Angels*, when she comes to realize what a devastating impact her beauty has on almost all the men whom she meets, she becomes arrogant and manipulative -- and again has to be admonished for her insensitivity. In *Dark Angel* she displays other sides of her character of which she would not be proud. She becomes besotted and obsessed with little Bry-

The old stile at the bottom of Greystone Hill, where one of the key episodes of "House of Angels" occurs

nach, and "loses" her own children emotionally. She does not even see their suffering for what it is. She becomes paranoid about The Nightwalker, and mistrusts those who are trying to protect her from herself. She interferes endlessly in other people's business, and throughout her life she displays a tendency for getting involved in mighty issues that would be best left to others to sort out. In *Rebecca and the Angels* she tries to tackle the tollgate grievances by becoming an honest broker or go-between, working with the Turnpike Trusts on the one hand and the small farmers on the other. In *Flying with Angels* she even tries to end the Irish Potato Famine by travelling over to Ireland with nothing in her bag besides good intentions! As she gets older she becomes more and more eccentric, and by the time she strikes up her relationship with Amos Jones, in the last ten years of her life, she seems actually to revel in her irresponsible and un-predictable behaviour, to the embarrassment of children and grand-children.

Occasionally Martha seems heartless when confronted by the suffering of others -- but we must not forget that Martha lives in an age which is brutal and in which death is very much a part of life. She kills three men (Moses Lloyd, Barti Richards and Zeke Tomos) with her own hands, and watches others die in horrible circum-stances. She also sends many other men to the gallows and to the penal colonies through her personal determination to see justice done. Vengeance -- rather than the tendency to deep depression -- is Martha's greatest demon. She agonizes about it in many sections of her dairies, wondering over and again whether she has allowed her noble and single-minded quest for justice to be transformed into a monster called "revenge". At times she knows that she has taken too much pleasure from the sight of a judge with a black cap on his head, and she recoils from what she sees inside her own mind. She is in-deed a heroine who is far from perfect -- and maybe that is why readers seem to love her as I do.........

The Five Ages of Mistress Martha

Martha's life can be divided up into five sections, which is why I de-cided that I needed five volumes to tell her story. If you look behind the adventures and the twists and turns of the storylines, I hope that you can pick up on the following:

In *On Angel Mountain* Martha is young and insecure, and has to learn very quickly to trust her own intuition and to take decisive actions on behalf of her family and the estate. She also has to learn how to survive. The story spans little more than one year, 1796-1797.

In *House of Angels* she learns what it means to belong to a fam-ily. Again the story is concentrated into a short period in the years 1805 and 1806. Martha has to cope with grief, widowhood and motherhood at the same time as assuming full responsibility for the running of the estate. And as she discovers what power she has over men she learns how to manipulate others and how to plan in detail the downfall of her enemies. In parts of this story, she is not a very nice person.

In *Dark Angel* she goes into another phase, again showing all too clearly the darker side of her character. She might still be beautiful, but without a man beside her she becomes uncertain, insecure and even paranoid. So in a sense she is discovering her vulnerability and learning a lot about herself. The story covers the years 1807 - 1822, but with two considerable gaps in the narrative.

The coastal cliffs near Pwllgwaelod with the open common of Dinas Mountain on the skyline. Not far from here, Martha and Owain have their passionate picnics........

In *Rebecca and the Angels* Martha is a mature and confident woman in middle age. She is still beautiful (and knows it) but the family have flown from the nest and she decides that she needs to do something to make the world a better place and to leave a legacy that her children and grand-children will be proud of. So for better or for worse she allows herself to be dragged into the Rebecca Riots. The story runs through twelve years, 1832 - 1844, with two gaps in the narrative.

In *Flying with Angels* our heroine is confronting the realities of old age and the prospect of death. Should she drift gently into respectable senility? Such a fate is not for Martha, and events conspire to pull her into a new relationship (with Jones the Prophet) and into conflict with church, chapel and the Secret Society of Sea Serjeants. She knows that she will not die in her bed. Nor does she -- but, true to form, she decides for herself how and when she will go to fly with her angels. This story spans ten years, 1845 - 1855.

A Tragic Heroine

I am often asked whether I intended, on embarking on the Saga, that Martha should be a classic tragic heroine in the mould of Desdemona or Antigone. Yes, I was aware that tragedy would be an ongoing theme, and that Martha's personality would be a trigger for truly appalling events.

Many centuries ago Aristotle wrote that the true tragic hero or heroine should be neither purely innocent nor purely evil. He or she should be high-born and should also possess a tragic flaw, originating from within and usually manifesting itself through poor judgment and maybe extreme arrogance. Arrogance may be the most dangerous characteristic, and since not many poor people are arrogant, that may lie behind Aristotle's idea that true tragedy was a prerogative of the upper classes! The "tragic flaw", which may or may not be obvious, also dooms the character to a ruinous and inevitable destiny and drags others down too. In a tragedy enacted on a stage, this should arouse pity in the audience, and the character should show that he or she is aware of what cruel fate has in store.

In writing about Martha's life, I did not have to work at the tragic components of the story. It was clear to me right from the beginning that as she travels through a long and exciting life she trails disaster in her wake. Her beauty is the source of her strength and also her curse, and as she survives one terrifying episode after another she loves and loses not just one good man but five. Many of her enemies love her too, or at least lust after her. In some ways she is naive about her own power over men; but her friends and family see it perfectly well, and do their best to warn her and protect her. There is an inexorable momentum in Martha's tragedy. In some way

Bluestone slabs near the summit of Martha's mountain

it is surprising that she survives into her seventies, but I knew before I tapped a single word of her story into my computer that while her men would all suffer miserable and gruesome deaths, she would go to her maker in a manner of her own choosing, and in a state of grace. So she goes to sleep on the top of her mountain, on a cold and starlit February night, and drifts away. Is that a suitable death for a true tragic heroine? You tell me!

Mother Wales

I did not realize it at first, but as the writing of the novels proceeded, I came to appreciate that Martha is actually Mother Wales, personifying all that is good and bad about my native land. As indicated above, my erratic heroine is feisty, passionate, very beautiful, willful, tending towards depression and even paranoia, fiercely loyal and protective of those in her care, idealistic, at times devious and manipulative, hard-working, generous and spontaneous, trusting, faithful and very determined and dogged. She does of course mature and grow more mellow as time goes on. I could go on --- I suspect that as author I do not see all of the vices and virtues that readers see. I am probably too close to her! But one of the key things about her, which I touched on in an earlier chapter, is her sense of *hiraeth* or belonging -- she really feels that the Plas and Carningli are a part of her, as she is a part of them.

A Scottish friend of mine pointed out to me some time ago that Martha Morgan is Mother Wales just as Chris Guthrie (in the three Grassic Gibbon novels) is Mother Scotland. I had never heard of Grassic Gibbon or the *Scots Quair*, so I bought the trilogy and read all three stories in rapid succession. I thought them quite brilliant. But I don't think that Gibbon liked Scotland very much (he portrays it as bleak, dour and mean-spirited), and his heroine is from beginning to end a peasant and a victim who reacts to events but hardly ever seeks to influence them.

120

Mistress Martha

There is no way that Martha is a victim -- she is a very different character indeed, and her relationship with the landscape is a love affair, from beginning to end. Maybe Welsh people do feel rooted in their landscape, in a way that is perhaps not fully understood by the Scots and the Irish. Wales has seen its share of troubles and traumas down through the centuries, but maybe they have not been as severe as those associated with the land evictions and rebellions of Scotland or the Potato Famine and the "troubles" of Ireland. Rural people have actually had to **flee** from the land -- and it was a hated land -- in Scotland and Ireland, whereas they have **chosen** to move away from the land in Wales -- either to the South Wales Coalfield or the Midlands during the Industrial Revolution, or to the United States and the colonies in search of a better life. I have tried to portray some of the pressures which pushed people to move away from the Welsh countryside, in the pages of the Saga. The keyword was choice, rather than compulsion, and it is a little theory of mine that those who left Wales travelled not with a hatred of a harsh land in their hearts, but a sad regret at having to leave behind a place of beauty. They sighed, and wept, and prayed that they might one day return. So the psychological relationship between people and land was different in Wales, and I have tried to show that in Martha's personality. When the land around the Plas is ravaged by floods or shaken by thunderstorms, or blanketed in snow, or frozen so solidly that work is well nigh impossible and animals die, Martha does not rage against a cruel God or against the vagaries of nature; she opens her eyes in wonderment, rolls up her sleeves, and tries to get the estate back to normal again.

I'm flattered that readers might think of Martha as Mother Wales. If I give my heroine assorted characteristics which are less than flattering, and if it is assumed that I see those characteristics in Wales and the Welsh, maybe I can get away with it since I am a Welshman myself!

But if readers then think that I have in mind the Five Ages of Wales, that might be going a bit too far......

6. Other Characters

It is never possible in a work of fiction, or even in five works of fiction, to explore more than a few characters in reasonable depth. Since there are more than 200 characters in the stories, it is inevitable that most of them will be shadowy figures, seen in detail here and there, but for the most part hidden behind the crossing strands of the stories as they develop. That is what happens in most books, and readers are generally quite happy to create their own mental pictures of those who come and go. There are some characters who, in retrospect, I should have spent more time on. David is one of those, and his daughter Betsi is another. I should have done more to develop the characters of some of the villains, including Alban Watkins and John Fenton, and one reviewer of the books has commented that in the stories the good people are too white and the villains are too black. I accept that criticism, and recognize that there should have been more grey in the portraits of Martha's enemies, on the basis that even the most wicked of men have some good sides and some characteristics that might be attractive. After all, Watkins loves his family and seeks to provide for them in the future, and Fenton is, in his better moods, charming and urbane.

So what of those whose characters I have developed quite fully in the stories? Here are a few notes about some of my personal favourites.

Joseph Harries the Wizard

Joseph Harries of Werndew is one of the key characters in the story. He was born in 1761 and died in 1826 at the age of 65. In Martha's time, wizards (or "knowing men") were greatly respected. Joseph

The old mortuary on the Parrog, where Joseph Harries Werndew has the terrible task of examining David's body following the fateful Cnapan game of 1806

Harries really did exist -- there are a number of folk tales about him. In reality, it seems that he might not have been a very nice fellow! And he did live at Werndew, just above the village of Dinas on the north side of the mountain ridge.   The cottage was, and still is, within walking distance of Carningli and Plas Ingli. But in my mind, and in the stories, Joseph is a herbalist, mystic, apothecary, surgeon, psychiatrist, sleuth, diplomat, counsellor and master of the arts of observation and deduction. He is a scientist, as well as being a man of culture. He knows several foreign languages and is familiar with many of the esoteric books on which the world's great religions are based. On occasion he retreats into his cottage before emerging, exhausted, with answers to very complicated questions; but there is always the possibility that he is a "charlatan" with a superior intellect and an ability to observe things and make deductions in the manner of a prototype Sherlock Holmes. Whether or not he is familiar with the denizens of the spirit world, he certainly does have a vast range of abilities, acquired during years of careful study under a variety of great teachers, whom he mentions every now and then. We cannot doubt that in some way he is the inheritor of the wisdom of the Druids, who were reputed to be active in this area at the time of the Roman invasion and who might have had a grove in Tycanol Wood.

Joseph is a stout and loyal friend to Martha, and a friend to many others as well. Sometimes he charges for his services, or overcharges in certain cases, on the basis that his services provided to the poor are generally free. So as well as being a Sherlock Holmes, he is also a Robin Hood figure, loved by the poor and hated by at least some of the rich. He is also Martha's knight in shining armour, who rides to her defence from his place across the mountain whenever he senses that she is in distress or in danger.

But while Joseph is always good humoured, eccentric, witty and supportive of others, he is also a tragic figure. As the stories unfold he reveals very little about himself and his family background, for as he explains to Martha, it is in his own interests to maintain an air of mystery about who he is, where he has come from, and where he will go to when his task on earth is done. But in one sensitive moment he admits to Martha that he was once married and that he lost his wife and child in childbirth. He dies after a horrible accident, gored by a bull during the course of a routine visit requested by one of the estates. There is irony as well as tragedy in that, since Joseph says many times that he enjoys working with animals. He loves Martha from the the very beginning of the stories. This might be suspected by the reader, but Martha never realizes it until Joseph confesses it to her when he is on his death-bed. Even then he can try to make light of it, and when he has gone to his grave Martha finds the situation very difficult to bear, blaming him for his foolishness in allowing his emotions to get the better of him, and blaming herself for her blindness as to the reality of the situation.

Joseph knows, from the beginning of their relationship, that his love for Martha will never be requited, because she is a member of the gentry and he is a disreputable wizard with nothing but a small cottage and a pretty garden to his name. In any case, he is almost old enough to be her father. So he loves and worships her from a distance, gaining comfort from their close and easy relationship, and some physical pleasure from their frequent embraces.

He is quite a mysterious figure, and by all accounts he has a little fan club all of his own!

Shemi Jenkins, servant

As an author I'm very fond of Shemi, because he is a seemingly simple fellow who works on the farm and who habitually uses his great strength in working with animals and in shovelling manure. He was born in 1782 into the Jenkins family of Blaenwaun, and he starts work at the Plas in the year 1797. He has a blossoming romance with Sian and marries her in 1810, going on to raise a family of his own. But he has hidden depths. The reader sees that he has special powers from the beginning, and this is recognized by both Martha and Joseph. One special talent is the ability to talk with animals, and if there are uncontrollable cattle or horses to be calmed, he is the man to send for. The Wizard of Werndew realizes quite quickly that Shemi will be his successor, and when Martha comes to appreciate his talents fully she agrees that he should go away for training as a wizard. So off he goes to study with Dr John Harries of Cwrt-y-Cadno. He comes back and takes over Joseph's work and his cottage, and from that point on he to becomes a sort of mentor for Martha, in spite of the fact that he is much younger than she. He features quite prominently in *Flying with Angels,* and the high point of his career comes in the terrible and comical episode in Brynberian Chapel when he turns the tables on the sanctimonious deacons who are seeking to excommunicate poor Amos from their congregation.

That is one of my favourite episodes from the whole series of novels, and perhaps this explains my affection for the character of Shemi.

Bessie Walter, lady's maid

Bessie is one of the key characters in the story of Martha and Plas Ingli. She is at the Plas when Martha arrives in 1796, and she is still there when Martha goes to her grave in 1855. She was born Bessie Gruffydd in 1776, and starts at the Plas in 1795. Later, after the adventures recounted in *On Angel Mountain*, Bessie leaves to marry the merchant Benji Walter in 1799. She then experiences tragedy after only three years of happiness, when she loses both her husband and small son in the year 1802. She comes back to the Plas as Martha's special servant, and is in that position position when David is murdered and during the period in which Martha has to survive as a young widow with a growing family, and at the same time must learn how to run the estate single-handed. So Martha's relationship with Bessie is forged in the fire, and becomes virtually unbreakable. At this time, when Bessie is in her prime, I picture her as very pretty and petite, with a strength born of hard labour in kitchen and harvest field. There are many men who desire her, and Dai Darjeeling remains madly in love with her for many years. She enjoys his attentions, and probably, away from the pages of the book, enjoys an interesting sex life when Mistress Martha is otherwise occupied. As the children grow older Bessie takes over as housekeeper in the year 1812. From that point on she becomes a fierce and efficient successor to the formidable Mrs Owen who was housekeeper when the Saga began.

It is to Bessie that Martha entrusts the last of her diaries, which are then found among her possessions long after her death at the age of 81. That is entirely appropriate, because the relationship between Bessie and Martha is in some ways more intimate than that between a wife and a husband. A lady's maid at the time of the stories would have spent a good part of every day in her company. She would have brushed her hair, laid out her clothes, scrubbed her back in the tin bath, made her bed, lit her fire every morning, emptied her chamber pot, and disposed of bloody rags at the times of her periods. She would have been with her in episodes of childbirth and times of grief. Little wonder then that Bessie should be more of a friend than a servant almost from the beginning of the stories. She hardly ever over-steps the mark, and she always shows due respect to her mistress, and a good deal of discretion; but she knows Martha almost too well, and is occasionally so impertinent that she risks instant dismissal. She knows Martha will not dismiss her whatever she may do or say, because she is absolutely invaluable; in any case, she is Martha's conscience.

When Liza takes over as Martha's personal maid, the two women never develop quite the same sort of relationship, partly because Liza has a husband and a life outside the Plas. So even when Bessie is housekeeper, she and Martha remain the closest of friends, and Bessie is normally that person whose duty it is to take Martha to one side and to tell her that she is behaving selfishly or unkindly towards other people. At times she is brutally honest, and at times even cruel, but because Martha loves her so much she is prepared to accept criticism from her in a manner that she would never accept from anyone else. The only other woman who has the temerity to admonish Martha occasionally is Grandma Jane in the early part of the Saga, but she speaks to Martha more as a mother would speak to a child, and that relationship has nothing like the same intimacy as that between Martha and Bessie.

Patty Ellis, prostitute

Patty Ellis appears for the first time in *House of Angels*, and becomes a key character in the stories from that point to on. Although she is a prostitute when Martha first meets her, the two women are immediately drawn into a close and affectionate relationship. It would have been socially quite unacceptable for the mistress of an estate in the early 19th century to have been seen in the presence of a prostitute, but it is one of Martha's great strengths that she cares nothing for wagging tongues and disapproving looks and soon after they meet she even flaunts her friendship with Patty. Initially the relationship might seem to be a very one-sided one, but there are in fact great mutual benefits in it. Patty initially offers to help Martha because she has information which is of use to her, and she has no thought at

The coastal community of Parrog, where Patty Ellis is forced into prostitution

all that she might be repaid in some way. But as the friendship blossoms, Martha realizes that Patty has suffered appallingly at the hands of the evil Joseph Rice, and she also comes to appreciate that Patty is a very strong young woman, with an instinct for survival.

So together the two women plot to achieve the downfall of Rice and his companions, and after that is achieved Martha and Patty develop a much more comfortable friendship. That friendship also has a business side to it, for as Martha gets older she comes to value greatly her contacts among the most disreputable elements of local society. She often needs information, and Patty often knows where it can be obtained. And as a sign of her affection - and indeed respect - for Patty, she helps her in a number of ways, including the setting up of the church wedding, when Patty and Jake Nicholas decide that they wish to be married.

Patty is of course very beautiful, and it is not surprising perhaps that Jake, who was originally at client, should fall madly in love with her and should then decide to make her a respectable woman. Their wedding is quite a bizarre, and Martha loves every minute of it and the celebrations which follow. Later on, as Jake expands his little fishing business and eventually moves into trading activities, Patty does indeed become a notable member of the Parrog community and raises a family of two boys and two girls.

I had a lot of fun developing the story of Patty and Jake through the Saga, telling the reader about her initial fall from grace, about her steely determination to defeat her tormentor, and about her subsequent rehabilitation. She is a strong character and a steadfast friend to Martha, and all good stories need characters like her.

Wilmot Gwynne, industrialist

Wilmot Gwynne breezes into the story in 1845, and plays quite a prominent part in *Flying with Angels* during the last ten years of Martha's life. In some ways he is a comic or a buffoon, and indeed he is part of the comedy duo of Wilmot and Delilah; but he is also much more than that, for as the story develops he shows that he is a multifaceted character. He is a rough sort of fellow, with very few airs and graces, who has made his fortune in the Swansea Valley through hard work and good judgement. He is a *nouveau riche* entrepreneur who moves into rural Wales for health reasons, and maybe also because he fancies the idea of being a squire rather more than being an industrialist. But he is generous to fault, and when he takes over the

The healing well at Llanllawer, not far from Plas Llanychaer, the grand house occupied (in my imagination) by Squires Price, Morgan and Gwynne as the story unfolds

Plas he shows great sensitivity in allowing Martha to remain in the house she loves and to maintain her status in the community. He could have sent her packing, and in the process destroyed her life and her family; but he chooses not to do that, maybe because like most of the other men in the Saga he is more than a little in love with Martha. As the final chapter in Martha's life unfolds, and moves inexorably towards its tragic conclusion, Wilmot again proves to be a steadfast friend to Martha, Amos and the Morgan family.

What does Master Gwynne expect as payback, after the provision of so much moral and financial support? Possibly some enhanced status in the community, which is what he needs in order to establish himself as a respectable squire. Maybe he is also seeking to demonstrate to his family and acquaintances that he has that almost indefinable quality called sensibility. That too, above all else, is what marks a member of the gentry out to from the mass of the population - and it is assumed very often in the literature of the day that sensibility comes only with good breeding, and cannot simply be acquired by those of low breeding who suddenly become rich.

Part of my purpose in developing Wilmot as an important character in the last story of the Saga was to demonstrate that, of all the members of the gentry who hobble or stamp across the pages of Martha's diary, Wilmot is one of very few who can truly be referred to as noble man. The others are Lord Cawdor, Richard Fenton, and John Bowen of Llwyngwair. Wilmot Gwynne, with his portly frame, calloused hands, and rough way of speaking, has every right to to sit at the same table as those famous characters from Pembrokeshire history.

Owain Laugharne, Martha's lost love

Owain Laugharne, the second great love of Martha's life, is more central to the story than husband David who dies in February 1805. He is a heroic and at the same time a tragic figure. Much of *House of Angels* is concerned with the tentative and tender progress of the love affair between Owain and Martha, and the story of their relationship is also a key part of *Dark Angel*. At the end of that story it appears inevitable that the two of them will be married; but of course that never happens and although Owain survives until 1825 he remains determined to the last that he will not to marry Martha and that he will not thereby remove the inheritance of the Plas Ingli estate from her children and grandchildren. Ironically, they fail to inherit it anyway, since the estate is lost in 1845. Owain goes through life with a rather warped sense of duty, and this is of course a great source of irritation to Martha. But she loves him with a fierce passion, and following his return from foreign parts she defies all of the conventions of good breeding by making it obvious to friends and enemies alike that the two of them have an unmarried intimate relationship. That causes considerable grief to the younger members of the Morgan family, who are more concerned about appearance and reputation than is Martha herself. (That is of course not the only occasion on which Martha's appetite for sex gets her into trouble. Next time round, apart from a dalliance with solicitor Hugh Williams which she gets away with, the lucky recipient of her favours is Jones Minor Prophet.)

So what lies behind Martha's great love for Owain? Well, he is a very interesting character. He is physically very attractive, as Martha admits at a very early stage in their relationship. She is deeply affected by the sight of Owain splashing about in the pool at Pandy, without a stitch of clothing on, and singing like an innocent child who has not a care in the world. That quality of innocence or naivete is perhaps the crucial feature of Owain's personality. He is cultured and sensitive, and has an extraordinary sense of decorum. He holds back when others might join in, on the basis that he is unsure about what might be deemed to be unacceptable behaviour. Even his sister Mary Jane, one of Martha's greatest friends, jokes about his exaggerated sense of duty and stiff demeanour. That irritates Martha as well, for in spite of her love for him she admits in the pages of her diary more than once that she would like to see more spontaneity and courage when he is with her on the social stage.

The crucial episode which demonstrates Owain's obsession with decorum and reputation is that in which he writes a letter to Martha before the party at Plas Glynymel. Martha misunderstands his behaviour, which is in reality entirely honourable, and as a consequence ends up drunk and in bed with the dastardly John Fenton. She is angry with Owain for what she sees as timidity and an obsession with appearances, and lives to regret her hasty misjudgment of the situation.

Since Owain is a poet, a musician, and a man given to sending flowers to his beloved, one might expect him to be blissfully unaware of the subtleties of convention and etiquette. After all, many great artists are so self-obsessed that they fail to see the consequences of their actions as they affect other people. So it would have been easy to build into his character wild eccentricities and outrageous deeds. But because he was a sensitive and quiet child, he turns out to be a very naive adult, and this is what underlies his timidity and dithering during the course of his love affair with Martha. And don't let's forget that Martha is a desirable young widow with a very

The interior of the little church at Pontfaen, adjacent to the big house occupied (in the stories) by the Laugharne family

young family, and that in the 19th century there are very strict conventions concerning periods of mourning and appropriate behaviour following the death of a husband. Although Martha may not always realize it, many of Owain's actions are motivated by his desire not to harm the children and always to treat them with affection and respect.

Courage is not something which Owain lacks. During the course of his life he shows an ability to survive the most appalling cruelty. In *House of Angels* he is terribly mutilated by the villains who believe that he knows the location of the Plas Ingli treasure. He survives that ordeal, although Martha suspects that it has harmed his mind as well as his body. Then, when he disappears for fifteen years out of Martha's life, he suffers again, tortured as a spy in the complicated wars that afflicted the European mainland in the early part of

133

the 19th century. We never really discover what terrors Owain had to endure, but we are quite certain that the damage was immense. Although he returns from foreign parts somewhat belatedly in 1822 on the night before Martha is due to marry Ceredig, and although she gives up that poor fellow for her old love, Owain has lost most of his youthful vitality and he is never the same again. For a year or two there is a brief passionate interlude in which Martha and Owain offend the sensibilities of the more respectable members of the community. She does not care, or at least professes not to care, and maybe Owain is too ill to care. The story of his sad decline between 1822 and 1825 is not told in detail, but of course it affected Martha very deeply.

But in the last few years of his life, Owen shows that he is strong enough, in spite of his physical weakness, to refuse to marry Martha. And it takes a very strong individual to stand up against the wishes of the Mistress of Plas Ingli!

In case anybody wondered, the story of Owain's long absence and eventual return probably came into my head because I was already familiar with an old Welsh folk tale which relates a similar occurrence in the Teifi Valley above Lampeter. On checking, I find that there are very similar stories in folk tale collections from other countries as well - so there is nothing particularly Welsh about this part of the story. What is unique, I hope, is the use of strong characters in the retelling of an essentially simple tale, and the emotional involvement of the reader in Martha's dilemma and in the tragic consequences of Owain's sudden reappearance.

Finally there is one question which I am often asked about Owain's behaviour. Why, people ask, does he remain abroad for fifteen years if he is genuinely in love with Martha? Why does he not move mountains, as a passionate and heroic lover, to return and claim her as his bride? The answers to those questions are provided to some extent in the pages of the Saga, but in his long explanation of his absence in the concluding pages of *Dark Angel* he describes how he picked up news (faulty news, as it happened) of Martha's marriage to another suitor. He knows that if he was to return to find her a married woman, that passion between them would be re-ignited, with the result that several lives would be destroyed. Like many tragic figures, Owain is also a martyr, and I think it is entirely in character for him to remain on the mainland of Europe, carrying his love for Martha like a great cross upon his back in the confident belief that in his suffering he is contributing to her happiness and to the well-being of her family.

Amos Jones, preacher and prophet

Amos Jones, itinerant preacher, minor prophet and last great love of Martha's life, is another character of whom I am very fond. He is, like Wilmot Gwynne, a product of his age. Wilmot comes from the white heat of the industrial revolution, and Amos comes from the white heat of religious fervour, as a man intent upon spreading the gospel and saving souls. He is an unlikely lover, for he and Martha have a wide social gulf between them, but they make immediate and easy contact when they first meet, and in some ways Martha finds him similar to her great friend and mentor Joseph Harries. Both Joseph and Amos are fiercely intelligent, radically inclined and lacking in respect for the establishment. They have a similar sense of humour, and speak in a way which Martha finds attractive. They are also instinctively drawn to fight against injustice and to help the poor. Maybe Martha has learned some lessons from her relationship with Joseph, which might have developed further had it not to been for his determination to hide his love, and to protect her from the challenges that would have accompanied an inappropriate marriage. Martha never says this directly to her diary or to anyone else, but maybe, as she felt drawn towards Amos emotionally, she thought "To hell with convention! Now I am going to live dangerously! " And live dangerously she does.

One of the reasons why Martha and Amos are drawn together is their shared awareness of the world of the supernatural - and that is of course one of the reasons why Martha and Joseph have a natu-

135

ral empathy for one another. But Amos combines a familiarity with ghosts and the other residents of the spirit world with a firm Christian conviction and devotion to his calling as a pastor and itinerant preacher. In an age when many of Martha's acquaintances specialize in self-indulgence, Amos specializes in self-denial and seems to take pleasure in suffering. This makes him into an ascetic or prophet, and it makes him a very unlikely companion for Martha, who is not particularly religious and who has a long history of conflict with the church and with various rectors over tithe payments and other church matters. But Martha has already had a flirtation with Methodism, and maybe she is excited by the idea that she might learn more about the nonconformist community and its system of beliefs as a means of self-improvement. She has had conflict with the Baptists before, but she does not set out in *Flying with Angels* to fight with these good people or to humiliate them. I have tried to portray Martha in this story as a more mature and tolerant figure than she was in her younger days, and as a person who genuinely wants to support Amos in his chosen and difficult calling.

The core episode in Martha's relationship with Amos, namely the episode in which she seduces him in Tycanol Wood, is one of the most crucial episodes in the whole of Martha's life story. What follows next, tragic and gruesome though it is, leads on to high drama and considerable comedy in the big meeting in Brynberian Chapel. In a book such as this it is always very difficult to juxtapose horror and comedy so closely, and I faced a challenge in writing it down. I am not sure that I have got the balance exactly right, but it was fine fun to try!

Like most of the other men in Martha's life, Amos is essentially a tragic figure, involved in a loveless and unconsummated marriage and trying to find contentment and even salvation through good works, preferably a long way from the home that he has set up with his frigid wife. Martha gives him happiness, and a good deal of pain as well. He loves Martha with an intensity which he has never experienced before, so that is a sort of fulfillment for him. As the story unfolds Amos realizes that it is his destiny to sacrifice himself in order to save Martha from those who have put a price on her head. He does make the ultimate sacrifice, having arranged things in such a way that his friends are powerless to stop him. So, as pointed out in Chapter 9 of the last book, he is a Christ-like figure who is too good to be allowed to live in an evil world. He has many weaknesses, and Martha is much stronger than he. His destiny is to attract enemies who feel threatened by his goodness, and to suffer an unpleasant death at the hands of vicious men.

Moses Lloyd, servant and murderer

Moses Lloyd, the villain of *On Angel Mountain*, is the disinherited third son of the old Squire of Cwmgloyn. He has a very murky past, which is gradually revealed as the story unfolds. He has a gigantic grudge against the world in general, and against the Morgan family in particular. He has upset his father and alienated his own brothers, but he refuses to admit to his own shortcomings and blames Martha and her family for his own miserable station in life. He feels that he has gentry blood in his veins and that he therefore deserves respect from those around him whom he considers to be inferior. They give him no respect, apart from the respect which is accorded to all of the servants at the Plas who know their jobs and who work hard, and as time passes his resentment grows deeper and darker.

He has committed truly sickening crimes against the Morgan family, and before the story starts he has already killed six people. He lives in a state of denial regarding all of his crimes, considering that the Plas Ingli fortune is rightly his, and that murder and arson are somehow justifiable as part of his strategy to take possession of it. He stays at the Plas only because he is quite determined to drive the family away from the house and to dig up the treasure which he has buried in the ground. He has a hatred of hard work and an instinct for a life of debauchery, and although he despises the labouring class he is happy enough to drink with those who belong to it

In a deep crevice near here, Martha dumps the body of Moses Lloyd following the confrontation in the cave

and to be involved in petty crime in the disreputable taverns of Newport.

He is probably mad even at the very beginning of the story, but he is not unattractive, and at first Martha is quite intrigued by him. He has striking eyes and strong features, and a bronzed and fit body. He is also well educated and well spoken. He is attractive to women, and he knows it. He believes that he is much more handsome and more cultured than David, Martha's husband, and therefore expects that it will not be too difficult to prise her away from the man to whom she is married. His problem, and indeed his tragedy, is that he then falls in love with Martha and becomes obsessed with the idea of possessing her. When she rejects him, and ultimately humiliates him in front of all of the inhabitants of the Plas, he flees, cursing the family that has given him shelter and work, and swearing that he will have his revenge. He also swears to himself that he will possess Martha, if necessary by force. With insane logic he also decides that he must cut Martha's face in order to destroy her beauty and thus destroy the source of her power over him.

Moses may or may not know that Martha has worked out for herself the extent of his evil, and he certainly underestimates the strength of her character. He cannot tear himself away from the Plas, and so he stays in the vicinity, living on and off in Martha's cave while he awaits an opportunity to fulfill his appalling ambition. The final scene of *On Angel Mountain* was a very difficult one to write, because I had to portray a pregnant woman in extreme danger and a man who is brutal and deranged - and who might sound rational but is actually quite mad. The explicit descriptions of the brutal sexual assault in the cave took me a very long time to get right, but on looking back I'm reasonably content with it.

Once Moses has been dumped into the cleft in the rocks by an exhausted Martha, he is gone but by no means forgotten, for the experience leaves Martha deeply scarred physically and mentally. She hates Moses for what he has done and what he has tried to do to her, and indeed she admits in her confession that she killed him intentionally, that she knows no remorse and seeks no forgiveness. But later her hatred is ameliorated to some degree when she discovers something about his childhood. There is madness in the Lloyd family, and Martha discovers that when Moses was young he was subjected to extreme cruelty by his father, and had expectations dumped upon him which he could not possibly fulfill. Whether a childhood destroyed by abuse is sufficient to excuse the villain's abominable behaviour is down to the reader to decide.

Daisy, the black sheep of the family

I have as soft spot for our Daisy, even though she is absent from most of the Saga. She is born in April 1801 as the second of Martha's four natural children. She has a difficult childhood, and Martha never fully realizes the extent to which the little girl is affected by David's death when she is still only three years old. She is effectively starved of affection whilst her mother becomes obsessed with baby Brynach, the foundling who arrives one night on the front doorstep of the Plas, and then with the mysterious Nightwalker who makes frequent appearances on the mountain.

In the year following David's death Daisy disappears, and Martha finds her in the cave, having had a premonition that that is where she would be. During that episode it becomes apparent to the reader that Daisy is a strange child who lives in a fantasy world and who is likely to create problems for her mother in the years to come. Indeed she does create major problems, and Martha loses her emotionally and has a series of disputes with her in the difficult years of blossoming womanhood. Everything comes to head when Daisy goes off to London, swearing that she will never see her mother again and that she will have no further contact with her home or her family.

After that, as one story follows another, we are occasionally made aware by Martha that she has news of Daisy; but in truth she has rumours rather than accurate information, and all her letters to her errant daughter go unanswered. Just as Martha loses her son

Dewi and her youngest daughter Sara she loses Daisy, and the pain of that loss is made more severe by the knowledge that she is still alive but quite disinterested in acknowledging either her roots or a mother's love.

Then, out of the blue, a fat lady in exotic clothes arrives without warning at the Plas. Daisy has returned, and Martha is overwhelmed. Her first instinct, as in the Biblical story, is to kill the fatted calf and to celebrate. The reunion between mother and daughter is told in quite sparse terms in the final pages of *Rebecca and the Angels*, but there can be no doubting the depth of a mother's joy. It turns out that Daisy has led an extremely disreputable and colourful life while she has been away in London, and in the most unexpected way she proves to know some of the most influential people in the capital city, within whose power it is to steer through Parliament an Act which will reform the hated turnpike trusts. She has cavorted with princes and bishops, among others. She has four children by different fathers, but she is still unmarried; and later on, in the pages of *Flying with Angels*, she finds true love for the first time in her life and marries Dr. George Havard, thereby becoming respectable.

Whatever the excesses of her life in London might have been, in the last book of the Saga Daisy is a reformed character and a loving and supportive daughter. When Martha commits her great indiscretion in Tycanol Wood with Amos Jones everybody else is appalled, but Daisy is thoroughly amused since this is a minor matter indeed when compared with some of the things she has seen and done in London. So things come full circle. The daughter with whom Martha fought so continuously and could not control in her teenage years now becomes the daughter who best understands her mother's eccentricities and her willful behaviour. That creates a mutual respect and a strong and loving relationship, and Daisy then plays a very important role in protecting Martha and advising her as she plays out the final act in her dramatic life.

Lone holly tree on the flank of the mountain, not far from Carningli Lodge

7. Great Issues of the Day

Traditionally, the great awakening of Western Europe is associated with the Renaissance, but that was a time difficult to define, just as it was difficult to locate geographically with any precision. There was certainly a flowering of culture across Europe at that time, but we still cannot say when it started and when it ended. The period from 1780 to 1850 (The Industrial Revolution) is much easier to define, but it was not simply a time during which manual labour was replaced by the use of machines. There were massive social, economic and political upheavals as well, not to mention periodic flowerings of religion. That is why it was so exciting for me to be given the story of Martha Morgan and to have it set precisely in this period of transformation. So what did happen during the lifetime of our Mistress Martha?

It was a quite extraordinary time in European history, for not only do we have revolutions in several European countries, including the French Revolution and the subsequent Napoleonic Wars, but there was also trouble in Ireland and across the whole of Great Britain. It was important for the authenticity of the stories that Martha and her families should be "caught up" in the great issues of the day; and given Martha's instinct for social concern, she would certainly not have been able to resist active involvement in various reform movements. Here are a few themes, building on the information already given in Chapter 2.

The Decline of the Gentry

Around 1800 the gentry were struggling to make ends meet, and many of the old estates were falling into ruin as the squires and their ancient and revered families desperately tried to maintain their status and contrived to live well beyond their means. This desperation, coupled with the obsessive desire to make good marriages and to acquire land, lies behind the behaviour of many of Martha's enemies in the stories. They are villains, certainly, but we must also try to understand why they behaved as they did - and as David tells Martha in the pages of *On Angel Mountain*, they were all small fish in a pond, and if they did not swallow up smaller fish, their fate would certainly be to be swallowed up by larger ones. So they borrowed money, often at very high rates of interest, and took many other risks with their estates. They put themselves into very tight corners from which they sometimes escaped, but on other occasions, as illustrated in the story of Brynach, debts might suddenly be called in and apparently successful estates might suddenly fail and appear on the open market.

Enclosures

One of the tactics which was used by the owners of the estates in the period covered in the Saga was to take possession of land which was previously deemed to be common land. In the area around Carningli most of the land was owned by the Barony of Cemais, so enclosure was not easy, but there were instances where it did occur. Mostly this would involve Acts of Parliament, and also a great expenditure of money by those who wished to enclose and improve land for agricultural purposes; but often the real purpose was not land enhancement or drainage but simply the increase of an estate's acreage and therefore its market value. In many cases, landowners did not bother with legal enclosures, but simply enclosed land by a process of slow accretion, digging ditches here and there and building hedges or walls in the hope that nobody would notice. This is what Squire Price does in the Saga, and in the process offends not only the Morgan family of Plas Ingli but also many of the commoners who have grazing and other rights on the common.

Enclosures on the edge of Carningli Common. Many of these enclosed fields date from the early part of the nineteenth century, and they have reverted back to wilderness again since the Second World War

Illegal enclosures often led to physical conflict between the big squires and the commoners who saw their grazing land being whittled away around the edges of the common. Ironically, some of the squires who were most inclined to enclose land illegally were the same men who used the law to evict landless peasants who had the temerity to put up *ty unnos* cottages as a means of ensuring the survival of their families. The leading lights in the community could more or less do what they wanted, because they were the landlords, the employers, and also the magistrate who sat in the petty sessions. When land disputes came up before one of the strange courts in Newport or in the sessions, it could always be arranged by the squires that they would escape without punishment. No doubt money sometimes changed hands in this process, but that was not always necessary, because in the elaborate system of debt recording and repayment which operated in Pembrokeshire, one good turn would always be repaid eventually by another. The Morgan family of Plas Ingli will have nothing to do with this sort of corruption, and Martha rages against it very often in the pages of the novels. Almost always, her instinct is to fight against the mutual support mechanisms of the squirearchy and to uphold the rights of the poor, even if this might damage the security of the estate and bring assorted dastardly squires close to apoplexy!

The Merchants are coming

In the early nineteenth century the squires were also having to cope with the rise of the merchant class, with local men from West Wales making new fortunes out of sea trading, and with others making their money from the new industries that were beginning to flourish

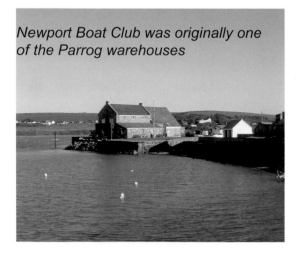

Newport Boat Club was originally one of the Parrog warehouses

to the east, in the coal mines of the South Wales Valleys, in the copper industry of Swansea, the tinplate industry of Llanelli, and the iron industry of Dowlais and other new towns on the edge of the Coalfield. Some of the new breed of industrialists, such as Wilmot Gwynne in *Flying with Angels*, move into North Pembrokeshire with money in their pockets, with great pretensions, and with a desire to acquire estates whenever and wherever they came on to the market. They could hardly expect to acquire land through marriage, because their daughters and sons were by definition not well bred and were therefore deemed "unsuitable". The fall of the gentry and the rise of the merchant class are inseparable.

Social Protest and Reform

While all of this was going on, there were other great stirrings in the social conscience of Europe, and this was reflected in North Pembrokeshire just as it was in other parts of rural Wales. The area may have been remote, but the squires and their families moved about quite widely, and books, newspapers, and pamphlets were available to all those who could afford them and who were prepared to think about the nature of society. So people like Grandpa Isaac, Joseph Harries and Martha herself would have been quite aware of the great issues of the day, including slavery, prison reform, voting rights, the defects of the justice system, and the conditions in the penal colonies. They, and many others of like mind, would have read literature that would have been considered subversive by the establishment; but they were still essentially loyal to the crown and would never have contemplated revolution, having read about the horrors that had been inflicted on all segments of society on the other side of the English Channel. But they did want reform, and it was down to people like the solicitor Hugh Williams and Martha herself to seek first to change the system from the inside, and if that did not work, through other means. There was a great debate in radical circles, for example within the Chartist Movement, as to the relative merits of violent protest and passive or peaceful protest. In the stories Martha, as a woman, instinctively seeks to change the evils of her world through negotiation and the use of female wiles, but she is not averse to the use of violence when all other means had failed. This is what lies at the heart of her involvement in the Rebecca Riots; she does not exactly condone violence but she goes along with it.

The Anti-slavery movement

The anti-slavery movement was in full swing during the period of the novels, but there was a very ambivalent attitude among squires and merchants about the slave trade and the value of human life. Although it is difficult to understand this today, those who lived in the period 1800 to 1850 had a very strange idea of what it meant to be human. Many intelligent people, encouraged by the media and by those who exercised power in Westminster, believed that the black people from Africa were scarcely human and that it was perfectly acceptable to treat them as commodities to be bought and sold. Some more enlightened people believed that they could be humanized or redeemed through education and contact with civilized people; and some actually believed that slavery was good for them in that it lifted them from a primitive jungle into an environment where they could indulge in honest toil and thereby improve themselves. Campaigners like William Wilberforce and Thomas Clarkson followed the lead of the Quakers and battled constantly against this sort of prejudice and blindness, and gradually won the day as more people came to appreciate the horrors of the slave trade.

And it could not be assumed that the churches were united in their opposition against slavery, for this was a period during which churchmen believed in the essential sinfulness of all men and women and the need for redemption. So it was easy for many of those who called themselves Christians to say that they were saved and that blacks slaves were not, and that primitive people were condemned by their own actions and their own life style to live in outer darkness. It is a source of shame to the church even today that church leaders from the period did not speak out against the evils of the slave trade and did not provide more moral support for those who fought for the freedom of African slaves in America and elsewhere.

It is also worth remembering that many of the squires and merchants who lived in North Pembrokeshire had shares in sailing vessels that were routinely used in the slave trade. They all made money out of slavery, and African slaves provided cargoes which were troublesome and dirty, but which nonetheless brought in a good income. And when times were hard, with estates teetering on the edge of bankruptcy, it would have been a risky matter for any squire to turn his back on such a lucrative business enterprise.

The Irish Potato Famine

The sort of attitude mentioned above also explains why the Irish famine was allowed to happen by the British government. If one looks at the literature of the day, including *Punch* and other magazines, we see a quite extraordinary and very distasteful portrayal of Ireland and the Irish, with Irish peasants in particular portrayed with ape-like characteristics in cartoons, and portrayed as trouble some and untrustworthy thugs in letters and reports from journalists. There were, of course, great political complexities to the Irish situation and to the terrible famine which afflicted Ireland between 1839 and 1845, but lying underneath the incredible inaction of the British political establishment and the apathy of most of the British public there was a belief that the Irish were too stupid to be saved from famine since they were too stupid to save themselves. After all, they lived on nothing but potatoes, they were Roman Catholics, and they had too many children. Could the famine and its traumatic and terrible effect on the people of that beleaguered country not be a sort of divine retribution visited upon a people which had gone astray?

In *Flying with Angels*, Martha learns a great deal about what is going on in Ireland from the families which come to North Pembrokeshire at the time of the harvest; and as indicated in Chapter 2 she is very distressed by what she discovers. She tries to arrange for assistance to go to Ireland for the poor starving peasants, but of course underestimates the complexities of buying, shipping and selling products that might be useful as food aid. She travels to Ireland herself to see what she can do, but discovers that her idealism is useless in the face of such intractable problems on such a vast scale. She becomes ill and has to return to the Plas; but she never forgives the government for allowing the Potato Famine to reach such tragic proportions, and for the rest of her life she becomes very sympathetic to the Irish cause.

The Chartists

During the first half of the 19th century, there was increasing unrest in Britain among the middle and lower classes since their lives were effectively regulated by men who came from ancient and wealthy families. They provided the Members of Parliament, and they were the only people who were permitted to vote. Gradually the franchise was increased to enable wealthy self-made men to vote as well, but that did not satisfy the masses who felt that their interests were never represented at government level. So radical movements sprang up all over Britain, some seeking to achieve reform and the extension of the franchise through lobbying and political activity, and others committed to violence and direct action. This was difficult for the government, and the Army was often called out to deal with trouble makers, to break up riots, and to bring subversive elements to justice. The most organized of the groups were those which went under the label of "Chartism". There were many strands and regional groupings within the movement, and some of the points that were made in the on-going debate are summarized in the pages of *Rebecca and the Angels.*

Nowadays we would consider the demands of the Chartists to be eminently modest and reasonable, but the politicians of the day appreciated that they were being threatened by a popular movement which, if it succeeded, would change forever the power structure of the country and would probably see them losing many of their seats in Parliament. Martha is of course entirely sympathetic to the Chartist cause, although she occasionally bewails the fact that those involved resort too easily to violence and fail to think out to properly what the consequences of their actions may be.

Smuggling

Trackway on the flank of Carningli. Tracks like this, well away from the town and the attentions of the Excise officers, were often used for the transport of smuggled goods

Smuggling was endemic around all of the coasts of Britain in the first half of the 19th century. Indeed it was considered to be something of a sport to run rings around the excise men whose task it was to find smugglers, confiscate smuggled goods, and bring those responsible to justice. That was not easy, because many of the magistrates in North Pembrokeshire and elsewhere depended upon the smuggling gangs to provide them with cheap gin, rum, wine and other alcoholic beverages, and also with whichever luxury goods happened to be subject to high taxation at any one moment. Taxation or "duty" was the key, and anything which was heavily taxed and therefore expensive to buy was immediately an attractive proposition from the point of view of those involved in the smuggling trade.

In Wales, smuggling was attractive to the poor people because it provided them with a trading opportunity, and therefore with cash in hand, at a time when there was very little cash in circulation. So they established links with merchants who were involved in the smuggling trade in the taverns of Parrog and Newport and provided the shore parties who would unload smuggling vessels at dead of night, spirit away the untaxed goods and then move them on to the middle men who would eventually dispose of them. There were many hiding places in the farms and cottages close to the coast and also in sea caves and in the woods. The men who were involved literally risked their own lives, especially if they were held to be responsible for injuring an excise man or a constable during an affray. Smuggling was also attractive to people like Martha, because they had no great love of the Westminster government and were only too happy to subvert the trading system and to assist in the distribution of illegal goods.

In the pages of the Saga there are a number of episodes related to smuggling and to the nocturnal activities of Will Owen and various other characters whom Martha counts as her friends. She gets too close to the action on one occasion, but she does not to seem to be unduly upset about it, and even after Will becomes a servant at the Plas she continues to be a good customer for products that might come onto the market at a good price, with few questions asked.

The System of Justice

The system of justice which operated across the United Kingdom in the decades before and after 1800 was so corrupt that it cried out for reform, and it is one of the on-going themes of Martha's diaries that she must fight against magistrates who use the law to maintain their own power base in the local community and to keep the poor people under control. Matters were actually very complicated in the ancient borough of Newport, because many disputes and offences were dealt with by the Court Leet, Court Baron and the View of Frankpledge. These archaic institutions, designed in the Middle Ages for the upholding of the law, were actually far more democratic than the Petty Sessions, because the men who served on them were burgesses, aldermen and freeholders; and they did have the ability, and the will, to punish members of the gentry on occasion. The mayor, appointed by the Lord Marcher, also enjoyed considerable power. However, with simplicity in mind, I have not allowed Martha in the stories to become involved with those courts because the explanations of procedures would have been far too complicated! So I have restricted my descriptions of the lowest tier of justice to the Petty Sessions, which were widespread and which supposedly operated according to a consistent set of rules. That is not to say that they were well regulated and honest. On the contrary, the manner in which they were run by the local magistrate was an outrage, and caused immense resentment not only among the labouring class but also among the rising class of merchants.

Although the magistrates were appointed on the recommendation of the Lord Lieutenant, and were in theory carefully vetted, the rules to which they were supposed to adhere were frequently flouted, and were in any case so vaguely written that those who sat on the bench could more or less do what they liked, and get away with it. There were hundreds of different offences which the magistrate understood only very imperfectly, and many apparently minor offences which actually carried the death penalty. There was no proper mechanisms, at least at the level of the Petty Sessions, for a defence case to be properly put, and there was no proper mechanism for appeal once a sentence had been passed. Things were a little better at the Quarter Sessions or Assizes which took place in the larger towns at regular intervals every year, but to the qualified judges and those who were put in charge of the administration of justice the erratic behaviour of local magistrates was a cause of constant irritation. Little wonder that a strong movement developed in support of sti-

pendiary magistrates who might at least know the law and who
might apply some consistency in sentencing policy.

In the Saga, Martha and many others of like mind are constantly angered by the vindictive and self-serving attitude of the

*Pentre Ifan old barn. In the stories this is the home of
the Rice family and the place where Martha experiences the workings of the Petty Sessions at first hand*

magistrates in the Newport area. This gets our feisty heroine into
constant trouble, but she will not accept a corrupt system, having
suffered herself from the ultimate humiliation of being stripped to
the waist and whipped through the streets of Newport behind the
whipping cart following a sham trial in the Petty Sessions. But she
has a deeper concern too, and that relates to the manner in which the
justice system is based upon the twin principles of harsh sentences
and Royal benevolence, as a means of controlling an increasingly
disaffected population of poor people. A death penalty might for
example be imposed for the theft of an article of clothing, after which
the condemned person would be encouraged to appeal to the King

for clemency. An appeal would be duly submitted, and after the prisoner had languished for some time in custody, the King in his infinite wisdom would grant clemency and commute the death sentence to transportation to the colonies. Very rarely there might be a full pardon. In this manner the law was used as a deterrent and the power of the state was maintained through the use of the Royal Prerogative. The condemned prisoner and his family and acquaintances were then supposed to be eternally grateful for a system which had built into it such magnanimity.

To their credit, there were many magistrates who had grave concerns about the operation of this system of justice in which property was given a greater value than human life, and they frequently refused to impose severe penalties on those who were simply trying to provide food for their children and who tickled trout or dug up turnips in their desperation. In the stories Grandpa Isaac and his enlightened cronies often give felons and others who have been charged with offences the benefit of the doubt, simply because they think that the evidence against them is thin or inadequately presented. Ironically this was another matter which brought the justice system into disrepute, with the level of proof required by one court being quite different from that required by another.

Penal Colonies

In the time of the stories, the prison regime was always harsh and often brutal. This is touched upon in Chapter 2. A spell in gaol often included severe physical punishment, so even if prisoners were not sentenced for the rest of their natural lives, many of them died from hunger, disease, medical neglect and excessive efforts, or during escape attempts. In the penal colony system, prisoners were deported far away to prevent escape and to discourage them from returning after their sentences expired.

Penal colonies were often located in so-called "frontier lands", and especially in the more inhospitable parts, where the unpaid la-

Water wagon in a reconstructed colonial settlement, Sovereign Hill, near Ballarat. Australia

bour provided by convicts could bring benefits to the colony before immigration labor became available. Even if there was regular immigration, as in Australia and Tasmania, the use of convicts by the new class of landowners held down their costs. There is no doubt at all that it was government policy (passed down to the magistrates and judges in coded language) that harsh sentences should be dealt out for trivial or dubious offences simply in order to generate cheap labour for the New South Wales colonies. And women were often sentenced on the flimsiest of pretexts, since the colonies needed prostitutes and wives.

The British government originally used North America as a penal colony through the system of indentured servants. Around 50,000 British convicts were banished to colonial America in the eighteenth century, representing perhaps one-quarter of all British emigrants. When that avenue was closed off in the 1780s after the American Revolution, Britain began to use parts of modern day Australia as penal colonies. Some of these early colonies were on Norfolk

Island (which became a "flogging hell" meant to deter even the most hardened criminals), then Van Diemen's Land (Tasmania) and New South Wales. Advocates of Irish Home Rule or of Trade Unionism (for example, the Tolpuddle Martyrs) often received sentences of transportation to these Australian colonies.

In his book *The Fatal Shore* Robert Hughes presents a searing indictment of the policies behind the setting up of the penal colonies, and of the manner in which they were run. The word "sadism" is hardly adequate to describe the gratuitous violence and the breakdown in civilization that occurred in certain camps. In *House of Angels* I have tried to describe just a little of what went on, and indeed the events in which Alban Watkins and the brothers of "Daniel O'Connell" were involved are based on real episodes. When Martha reads about Watkins' behaviour in Australia, and about his subsequent "execution" she is almost terrified out of her wits. Educated people who did receive news of the penal colonies became increasingly concerned about them on humanitarian grounds, and became convinced that the policy of exemplary punishment meted out to people who had been shipped to New South Wales at the whim of the magistrates was bound to have a brutalising effect on all who lived in and around the convict settlements.

Liberal opinion was gradually mobilised. For example, the *London Quarterly Review* published an article in June 1841 which included this statement: "Captain Maconochie condemns the whole of the penal institutions of the colonies, and says that the bad state of society may be traced directly to their pervading and demoralising influence; he complains that physical coersion (by which he means flogging) is resorted to upon every little breach of regulation .... in short, he says, in so many words, that the settlers who have convicts assigned to them are slave-holders, and the assignees slaves."

After a great debate in the UK, transportation to the colony of New South Wales was officially abolished on 1st October 1850, and in 1853 the order to abolish transportation to Van Diemen's Land was also made. But the abuses which were going on in the convict settlements went on for a long time after that, as attested in the story of Ned Kelly and many other bushrangers; and some will say that Australia has still not fully recovered from this murky episode in its history.

The Rebecca Riots

The Rebecca Riots, described in some detail in *Rebecca and the Angels*, took place between 1839 and 1844 in West, South and Mid Wales. They were essentially a protest against the high tolls which had to be paid on the local turnpike roads. (The term "turnpike" was used for a gate on which sharp spikes were fixed, originally as a defence against cavalry.)

The many toll-gates on the roads of West Wales were operated by trusts which were supposed to maintain and improve the roads and extend the road network. Many of them charged extortionate tolls and diverted the money raised to other uses. Even where this was not the case, the toll-gate laws imposed an additional financial burden on poor farming communities, and at last people decided that enough was enough. They took the law into their own hands and gangs were formed in conditions of great secrecy to destroy the toll-gates.

These gangs became known as Rebecca's Daughters (in Welsh: *Merched Beca*) or merely the Rebeccas. The origin of their name is said to be a verse in the Bible, Genesis 24, verse 60: *And they blessed Rebekah and said unto her, Thou art our sister, be thou the mother of thousands of millions, and let thy seed possess the gate of those which hate them.*

It is one of the great folk traditions of West Wales that the leader of the first riot, one Thomas Rees (Twm Carnabwth), wore women's clothes and a blackened face as a disguise when leading the attack. One could be hanged for rioting in those days, and certainly self-preservation was a priority for the rioters! But as indicated in the pages of Martha's diaries, the tradition of the *Ceffyl Pren* must have been knowingly incorporated in to the new "tradition of Rebecca's Daughters". Twm was the first Rebecca and he and his friends destroyed the toll-gate at Efailwen in 1839. Other communities then adopted the name, and the disguise, and as the rioting spread, other grievances besides the toll gates were aired by the protestors. For example, while squires were the main targets, clergymen from the established Church in Wales were attacked on several occasions because of the unpopularity of tithe payments and other ecclesiastical benefits. Other victims of Rebecca were petty villains such as the fathers of illegitimate children.

The riots ceased after several waves of protest, during which a very effective "grass roots" operation led the constables and the army a merry dance across a hostile countryside. Very few of the protestors were ever caught. The riots were ultimately successful, and they prompted several reforms, including a Royal Commission into the question of toll roads. Most of the hated toll-gates were legally removed in 1844 and a fairer system of toll charges was brought in.

In Part 4 of the Saga, Martha is middle-aged and decides that she wants to do something to save the world, or at least to make it a slightly better place. So she gets involved in the Rebecca Riots, more by design than chance.

There have always been unanswered questions about certain aspects of the riots. For example was there a single leader who orchestrated everything from behind the scenes? And if so, was that leader Hugh Williams the solicitor? Were the riots spontaneous, or were they organized well in advance by people who knew a lot about planning and secrecy? And was there a strong political motivation to the riots? In giving Mistress Martha a key role in one of the most interesting episodes in Pembrokeshire history, I have been able to have much fun by mixing fact and fiction and by suggesting that there might have been a female component in the planning of the riots. If Martha had been around at the time, she would surely not to have been able to resist the opportunity to have some fun at the expense of those who wielded authority.

I should mention again here (although I have also spelled it out in the relevant book) that the novel should in no sense be read as history. Because of the demands of storytelling, I had to invent a few turnpike trusts and a few riots...... and maybe I have even invented a few more spies than there were, and built in a little more treachery and mayhem.

The Evangelical Revivals

During the 18th and 19th centuries Wales experienced a succession of extraordinary surges of religious fervour which are generally referred to as the religious revivals. The first of these was the Methodist Revival initiated by John Wesley and his contemporaries, but after that a succession of evangelical preachers stirred the soul of the nation and led to a shift in the balance of power from church to chapel. Thousands flocked to great preaching meetings in the open air. New congregations sprang up everywhere, and new chapels were built in towns and villages and in the countryside. Among the nonconformists there were convoluted debates about theology, and new hymns were composed and sung with gusto. If one looks at the dates of the revivals, they seem to have occurred approximately every 20 years, not always with equal fervour and not always in the same part of Wales. In the early part of the 19th century there were certainly itinerant preachers like Jones Minor Prophet, and there were certainly wild outpourings of religious enthusiasm which sometimes bordered on hysteria. In *Flying with Angels* Martha feels awkward in the presence of people who profess too loudly that they have been saved through the sacrifice of the Lamb, just as she is uncomfortable about the complacency of the Church in Wales. But for better or for worse she gets caught up in the spirit of revivalism -- because she loves Amos.

We should not imagine that revivalism affected everybody in Wales. Even at the height of the great revivals there was a lot of sin around, and many thousands of ordinary folk were quite unmoved. But we should remember that there is a long history of spiritual revival in Wales, beginning in the third century and continuing to the present day. This history has its own unique spiritual heroes including Saint David and Saint Brynach, William Morgan with his transla-

The Church Chapel, Newport, built originally for the Methodists following the great eighteenth-century Methodist Revival

tion of the Scriptures into the Welsh language, Howell Harries and Daniel Rowlands (who were contemporaries and co-workers with Whitfield and Welsey in the 18th Century Methodist Revival), William Williams Pantycelyn, the famous writer of hymns such as *Cwm Rhondda*. Between them, these heroes under God transformed and changed a whole nation into one of the most Christian countries in the world by 1850 – so much so that the little nation became known as The Land of Revival **and** The Land of Song!

A number of themes have been highlighted by those seeking to explain the Revivals. One was the concern among Welsh industrial (and rural) workers over the apathetic attitude of the established church towards their poor living and working conditions. Another was the concern, especially among the Nonconformists, over the religious and moral decline of the working people. There was also a conscious attempt, in periods of "apathy", to do something about falling chapel memberships and attendances; to challenge the onset of Darwinism and modern, non-Fundamentalist Biblical criticism; and to resist the growth of agnostic Welsh socialism. Chapel elders were also making a conservative response, in a puritan tradition, to an increase not only in drunkenness, swearing and gambling, but also in the theatre, dancing, and rugby football. This is one typical statement: "Everybody who has taken a little trouble to observe the condition of the country must agree that there was a heart-breaking sight to be seen before the commencement of the present Revival. Most people seemed to have given themselves up to the Devil. Agnosticism had raised its ugly head very high. There was a terrible apathy inside the chapels and churches. The workers had fallen into a state of frightful callousness, and the whole country had descended into a pit of corruption. Lust and drunkenness, worldliness and worthless things had possessed the minds of all people."

It would seem, simply, that every now and then the power of the Revival Tradition became stronger than the combination of socialism, immorality, Darwinism, and dissipation which so horrified the faithful. Despite the changes in behaviour and the political aspirations of the social groups that had been the traditional backbone of non-conformism, over and again the revivals burned like wildfire across the Welsh countryside before things returned more or less to normal. In the pages of *Rebecca and the Angels* and *Flying with Angels* I have tried to flag up the importance of the revivals and the chapel congregations to which they gave birth. They were undoubtedly great places for socializing, education, and for the improvement of self-esteem and self-reliance, since chapel members were actually involved in decision-making. That was revolutionary in itself. But on the downside the congregations were very sanctimonious and very judgmental of others, and people like Martha were infuriated with them for the manner in which they accepted suffering and poverty as things ordained by God (or even as retribution for past sins), and for their failure to support those who worked hard for political and social reform.

The Circulating Schools

Griffith Jones of Penboyr founded the Circulating School movement in Wales as a way of reaching a greater number of children -- and also adults who could not read or write. His first school was established in Llanddowror in 1731, and then he began to develop further

Plaque on the site of the old school, College Square, Newport

small village schools run by itinerant teachers. The idea proved hugely successful and it has been estimated that around 3,500 schools had been set up by the time of Griffith Jones' death in 1761. Teaching was mainly basic literacy through religious texts provided by the SPCK, and charitable funds were spent on the teaching and not on buildings. Schools were run in barns, storehouses and other spacious premises. By the end of the century problems with securing adequate charitable funding caused the movement to peter out, but not before an appetite for learning had been created.

That led to the rise of Sunday Schools in West Wales. Classes were held on the day most people were available, and adults and children alike were invited to attend. The classes were held before or after the church services. Again, basic tuition in reading and writing was based on the scriptures. The success of the movement led to its adoption by all denominations and a new publishing industry came into being to satisfy the need for books. At first the schools were held in houses and barns. Later they were often held in purpose-built Sunday School buildings alongside churches and chapels, and funded by subscriptions and collections. Like the Circulating Schools, the church-based Sunday Schools created a huge impetus towards universal education and also gave support to the Welsh language.

As far as the Newport area was concerned, there were difficulties in finding premises and teachers around the time of the French Invasion. The episode described in *On Angel Mountain*, when the Circulating School comes to the Plas, would have been typical. But the movement was revitalized after 1804 when a large bequest from the movement's great benefactor, Madam Bevan, was "unfrozen" by the courts. That led to the building of Madam Bevan's College on College Square, and to the appointment of a full-time Master, whose name was John Morgan. He remained in his post for 45 years, until shortly before his death in 1865.

Benevolent Societies

The True Briton Society, which Martha supports in her early years at the Plas, really did exist. It was one of hundreds of small "mutual societies" or "benevolent societies" set up as a means of helping the poor. They were usually founded and run by well-meaning gentry wives, and labourers and servants were encouraged to use the societies and to save regularly so they they would have lump sums available when they needed them. Loans could also be issued, at favourable rates of interest, and grants could also be made at the discretion of the trustees. The main benefactors donated considerable sums of money to the larger societies, and these funds were sometimes used for the support of education or any other objectives specified in the governing documents.

Some of the more enlightened squires supported these mutual societies, but others hated them, and the episode described in *On Angel Mountain*, when Martha and her friend Ellie Bowen attend a meeting of the True Briton Society and greatly offend Squire and Mistress Howell in the process, is just one example of this.

Secret Societies

As explained in a note on page 38 of *Flying with Angels*, the Society of Sea Serjeants really did exist. It originally attracted gentlemen who had Jacobite sympathies, and was at its strongest in the eighteenth century. Later on it portrayed itself as a social and sociable club for gentlemen and their families, and it held meetings and outings to the seaside which were not particularly secretive. They were even reported in the local newspapers. But it was also a "mutual support" organization which promoted the interests of the local squires through price fixing, trade deals and political pressure behind the scenes. So there was another layer of activity, and in spite of its public face there was much that went on underground, or at least behind closed doors. I have not been able to discover anything about its rituals or about the obligations placed on members.

So the Society of Sea Serjeants was a "secret society" like the many others, including the Freemasons. It was therefore viewed with suspicion by non-members. It is reasonable to assume that at least some of its activities were corrupt and that it encouraged certain types of criminal activity. Whether it went so far as to hire assassins, and to systematically remove or eliminate those whom it considered to be enemies, is another matter!

Foxglove, beautiful but deadly. This was the source of the digitalis used to poison poor old Elijah Collins at the behest of the Society of Sea Serjeants

8. Symbols

Quite deliberately, the books are full of symbols. Some of them are intentional, and others have appeared in the pages of the Saga without any planning on my part! But if readers wish to see symbols where they were not intended, that's fine by me. In this short chapter, I want to mention some of the more obvious things that might have significance for the purposes of the story and for the understanding of Martha's character in particular.

Plas Ingli is the "quiet core" of Martha's life, and the place where her angels (family and friends) dwell. So, as mentioned earlier in the book, it is her House of Angels.

The Mountain

The mountain is her cathedral, dominating her world and her consciousness, just as the towers of Durham Cathedral and the mighty spire of Salisbury Cathedral dominate and almost intimidate the little houses and streets in the world below, reminding both God-fearing and godless folk that they are being watched and that they had better be careful. Martha is never frightened of her mountain, and never sees it as a place occupied by some vengeful deity, but she thinks of it as an extension of her own personality and as something high and beautiful which gives her strength. She never articulates this, but she feels that the hard blue rock gives strength to her muscles, and that the fresh air which she inhales is first purified and exhaled by the mountain. Mistress Martha, given life and strength by Rhiannon, the Earth Goddess? That might be going too far, but right from the beginning I knew that Martha had to die on the mountain summit, that the mountain would be convulsed by an earthquake at

The western summit of the mountain

the moment of her death, and that the summit profile would then be inherited from her profile when she was found by Will, Gerallt and the other men on the following morning.

The Cave

Martha's cave (there is obvious sexual symbolism here) is her sanctuary and her altar. Caves are revered in many societies (such as the old Guanche society of the Canary Islands) as symbols of fertility, and are even associated with fertility rituals. Martha describes hers in some detail which decorum forbids me to repeat just now. But if you must, look at page 55 of the first novel! The cave is also, in a sense, the womb, her special place of darkness and peace, which is why she is so outraged, in *On Angel Mountain*, that Moses Lloyd has defiled it. It is the scene of her most terrifying physical ordeal, and the place where, somehow, she finds the super-human strength needed to defeat and even kill her tormentor. For months and years after that, she cannot return to the cave, but at last (with Joseph's help) she does find the strength, and thereafter it is restored to its proper sanctity. The only other people who ever find the cave are Daisy, who is led to it (by the angels of the mountain?) when she is lost, and Iestyn, at the climax of *Dark Angel*. He is also led

Crags and tumbled boulders on the flank of the mountain. Martha's cave was near here

to the cave by an angel, and this time the angel is Martha.

At the end of *Flying with Angels* the cave becomes a tomb, for Martha decides that that is where the body of Amos Jones will be laid to rest. The menfolk from the Plas take his body there, in a slow funeral procession, and after placing him inside a big stone is rolled across the entrance. That is another obvious symbol! Martha says that she will never visit the place again, nor does she.

The Spring

*The spring on the flank of Carningli
which might just be Ffynnon Brynach*

The spring is a symbol too, and it is there that Martha performs her little rituals of drinking the crystal-clear water and anointing herself with it. The water refreshes and purifies. Ffynnon Brynach provides sacred and healing water for the Plas, reinforcing the sanctity of the house. When Moses defiles the spring by destroying the pool and dismantling the piped overflow, Martha attaches an almost religious significance to his actions. "Desecration!" she cries, and her sense of outrage compounds her determination to bring the villain to justice for crimes which she -- at that stage -- only partly understands.

The Ravens

The ravens are symbols -- not (as in Teutonic mythology) symbols of death and darkness, but as in Celtic mythology symbols of nobility, royalty and assorted other virtues such as steadfastness and protectiveness. The ravens are the spirits of the mountain, and although they are black they are really the mountain's "host of angels". Martha is very fond of them. Sometimes she pays attention  to what they are telling her, and sometimes -- because she is preoccupied with her petty obsessions and fails to read the signs -- she disregards them and pays the price. At the very end of the Saga , following Martha's death, six ravens appear on the mountain and watch as her body is carried back to the Plas. They are of course the spirits of Martha and her five men -- David, Ceredig, Owain, Joseph and Amos. Maybe Iestyn should have been there too, to make the number up to seven.........

The Kitchen Table

Then there is the kitchen table, solid and unmoving, the place where many of the dramas of the novels are played out. If you like, you can see it as an altar -- a place where bread is broken and wine is shared. It is the real centre of affairs -- a place of discussions and disclosures, meal-times and fellowship, life-saving operations, and even the examination and preparation of corpses. Here Martha dispenses orders and advice to others, and sometimes receives admonishment in return. The kitchen table is the place where, in volume 4, Zeke tries to rape Gwenno, and where he is almost blown to bits by Martha. So there is blood here too, in addition to bread and wine. But it is blood spilt in retribution, and not in self-sacrifice.

The edge of the grove in Tycanol Wood, where a great deal happens

What else?

Well, the grove in Tycanol Wood, where Martha makes love with a number of different men during her long life, is a place both sacred and profane, and a place of ecstasy and terror. Bessie, if you like to see it this way, is Martha's conscience. Jones Minor Prophet is a Christ-like figure, too good to be allowed to survive -- and he ultimately sacrifices himself to save others. The old traditions like the Wren House, the *Ceffyl Pren* and the *Mari Lwyd* are replete with symbolism. Some have seen symbolism in dates and numbers -- there may be symbols there, quite unbeknown to me.............

Yes, there are many symbols in the books, although I have tried not to cram in so many as to make the stories into allegories or parables.

9. The Supernatural

An old woodcut of a witch, a demon and a wizard flying through the air. By the early nineteenth century belief in such events was not widespread, but people were quite prepared to believe in "special powers" and ghostly happenings

From the very beginning, it was obvious to me that Martha had to have "special powers" just as certain families in this area are reputed to have special powers today. So she has heightened awareness and intuition, as well as experiencing visions and seeing omens that others miss. Shemi also has special powers, and eventually takes over

Joseph Harries's mantle (literally!). Episodes like the Battle in the Sky are recorded historically from this area, and of course corpse candles, phantom funerals etc feature strongly even in today's local folklore. So the things experienced by Martha would have been by no means unique. I've tried not to go over the top on this, but it adds an interesting dimension to Martha's character -- when she knows things that others do not know, and has to learn how to deal with this unsettling knowledge.

It's also important to the development of the Saga's storyline that the rest of the community (a simple rural community free of urban cynicism!) accepts as "facts" the supernatural encounters reported by others. We must not forget that, at this time, there was a belief in the literal truth of the Bible, and that people did not ask

The indistinct figure of The Nightwalker, a key player in "Dark Angel". Was he a man, a ghost or a demon? In the early nineteenth century, people would have been prepared to accept any one of these alternatives.......

fundamental questions about the reality of heaven and hell, ghosts and phantom funerals, and other supernatural phenomena. We must also remember that the Saga is set in the decades before the rise of scientific thinking. With rare exceptions, people did not indulge in the process which we nowadays refer to as deduction, and Darwin had not yet written his famous book called *The Origin of Species*. So it would have been perfectly natural for people to discuss supernatural things in an open and unpretentious way, and to have accepted without question what other people reported to them about strange sightings and strange events.

I have often been asked whether the occurrence of the supernatural in the Angel Mountains stories is an attempt on my part to cash in on the popularity of the Harry Potter books. The answer to this is that there is no relationship between Martha and Harry Potter, and that the occurrence of supernatural events in the story had come into my head well before the Harry Potter books began to make an impact in the UK. When Mistress Martha "came to me" during my strange feverish episode, I knew immediately that she had to have special powers, and that premonitions and supernatural phenomena would figure strongly in the development of the story. I also knew that Joseph Harries Werndew had to be in the stories as Martha's mentor and friend; he really did exist, and he really was a wizard. I also wanted to show how wizards and witches were not just tolerated but often respected as healers, herbalists, sleuths and amateur psychiatrists in the days before Charles Darwin and the development of modern science. The idea of "the knowing one" is very important in the Welsh folk-tale tradition, and I wanted to remind readers of that fact.

Phantom Funerals

There are many stories from all parts of Pembrokeshire about the sightings of phantom funerals, which were always assumed to be warnings to the community that a death would occur in their midst in the near future. Very often the sighting would be by only one person, who would see a funeral procession approaching, or passing by along a familiar route. In most of the stories the observer is initially convinced that he or she the is observing a proper funeral, and then the realization comes that this is indeed a phantom funeral which is the precursor of some family tragedy. In some of these stories which appear in Pembrokeshire folk tale collections, there is extraordinary detail about the makeup of the funeral procession, including faces which are recognized, the identity of the preacher and the person driving the hearse, and even details of clothing. And of course, when the real funeral then occurs maybe a week or a fortnight after the observance of the phantom funeral, these little details are replicated exactly.

In one famous story of a phantom funeral observed close to Cilgwyn Mill, Mrs Davies, an old lady who lived at the mill, actually observed her own funeral, and had to squeeze up against the hedge in order to allow the procession to pass. Afterwards she described to her daughter many quite extraordinary details of the procession and was so upset by the experience that she took to her bed and went downhill very rapidly. Within a few days she was in her grave. According to her family, the details of the phantom funeral which she had recounted were replicated exactly when the funeral procession passed from Cilgwyn Mill on its way to Caersalem Chapel where the burial took place.

In some cases, the details of a phantom funeral made it quite possible to know which person in the local community was destined to die in the coming days or weeks. Perhaps he or she was already very ill or very old. The observer would always recognize the minister and the family at the head of the phantom funeral procession, and that would give sufficient notice as to the name of the doomed person. However, there was also a convention that the observer would not talk too widely about to what he or she had observed until the death had actually occurred and the real funeral was over and done with. Then the tale would be told about the phantom funeral, and wide-eyed listeners would nod their heads in recognition that something significant had been observed, and maybe in recognition of the observer's special gifts.

Corpse Candles

There are many stories about corpse candles from all parts of Pembrokeshire. The corpse candle was a small light which might be seen passing along a lane, or in a graveyard. It was generally assumed that if a moving light was observed, that would be the route to be followed in the near future by a funeral procession, and if the light was seen in a graveyard it was assumed that it would hover at the place where a grave would be dug and where a burial would occur. There are number of stories from the Gwaun Valley about corpse candles, the best-known of which relates to a burial in the church yard of Llanychllwydog.

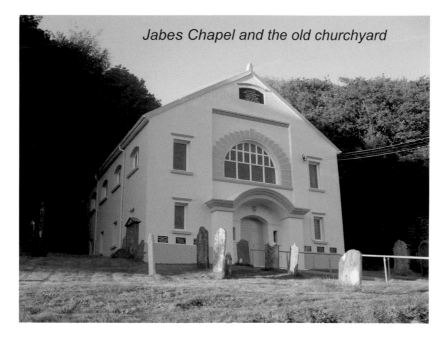

Jabes Chapel and the old churchyard

The observed light was generally very small, about the size of a candle flame. Most often it would be white but in other cases folk stories refer to blue, green or red flames, and the sighting of a coloured flame would generally be assumed to be the precursor to the death of someone very special, such as a local wizard or witch or even a member of the royal family.

When one looks at the stories of corpse candles in the county's folk tale collections, it is difficult to work out to whether the observers are perfectly ordinary people, or whether they are somehow selected for the sighting or are in possession of some special powers.

There is one famous example of a woman who lived near Jabes churchyard in the Gwaun Valley who saw corpse candles very frequently in the churchyard and who could accurately predict which members of the local community would die, and when. She was referred to locally as Hettie Howells the Visionist, and she lived around 1875.

Aderyn y Gorff

Loosely translated, this means the corpse bird, and in view of its macabre associations one might think that it should be a species associated with death and destruction, like the crow or a bird of prey. Not a bit of it -- in the Welsh tradition the corpse bird was small and brown, rather like a sparrow or a wren. In some of the old stories it is described as being grey in colour. The encounter with this unpleasant little bird was often a very insignificant thing in itself. For example, a person who was doomed to die might experience nothing more than a small bird tapping at the window pane for one night, or possibly for several nights in succession. That would be strange in itself, because of course small birds do not normally fly about at night. Sometimes the little bird would fly in through the front door of a house and into a room in which someone was destined to die. Although the corpse bird had dark associations, it was difficult in the normal run of the events for a person encountering a little bird fluttering inside a cottage or house to know whether any great significance should be attached to the event, since little birds are commonplace in country districts. Maybe the interpretation placed on an encounter with a sparrow or other small brown bird depended upon ones state of health, mental or physical. In my reading of the old stories, it appears that the bird would sometimes be seen by the doomed person, or sometimes by a member of his or her family.

I have always been intrigued by this particular supernatural phenomenon, probably because it is so unusual and so ordinary. I have used it in the Saga towards the end of *Flying with Angels*, and the person who sees the *aderyn y gorff* is Amos Jones, who is a student of the supernatural and who knows that this is a sign of his imminent death. He accepts that with equanimity, because he knows already that his enemies are out to to get him, and because he is already formulating a plan which will lead to the final tragic confrontation with the horsemen in Tycanol Wood.

The Battle in the Sky

This is something which is not unique to Wales. There are stories of battles being seen in the sky from all over the Western world, and it appears that those who see them are always very frightened by them. Their descriptions of what they have seen and heard are often very detailed, with specific mentions of the sounds of weapons flashing, men screaming, horses neighing and falling to the ground, and clouds of arrows flying through the air. There are not very many stories of battles in the sky actually being observed in Wales, but in my researches I have come across three stories from North Pembrokeshire. All three of them come from the area around Mynydd Morfil and Puncheston. Interestingly enough, in each of the stories the battle was observed by more than one person, and on one occasion the battle was seen above Morfil by two gentlemen who were very frightened by it and who sought refuge in a nearby house. They were given shelter as the battle continued in the sky, observed by the two refugees and by the householder. A feature of these phantom battles is that they seem to be quite prolonged, maybe continuing for more than two hours, whereas most supernatural phenomena appear to come and go within a few minutes or even seconds.

It is difficult to tell from the literature whether phantom battles are spiritual recordings of something which has happened in the past, or whether they are omens or signs of some tragedy to come. When Martha encounters her battles in the sky in the stories, she is in no doubt at all that they are supernatural indications of some tragedy which will soon affect her or those whom she loves -- and of course she is right.

There is much speculation about the occurrence of the battle in the sky in the heavens above Mynydd Morfil, but historians now seem to agree that the location is precisely right for a famous and bloody battle which occurred in the year 1087 when two Welsh armies met. The conflict was really just part of the internal power struggle within Wales following the Norman invasion. The Normans were already moving into Wales, and if the Welsh princes had then united instead of fighting each other, the history of the Norman invasion (and of Wales) might have been quite different. One army, which included many mercenaries from Ireland, landed at Porthclais near St David's and marched eastwards for one day. The other army, assembled by an alliance of Welsh princes, was marching westwards from Cardigan. Thousands of soldiers fell in the battle, which had no obvious victor -- so it was ultimately quite futile. It was called the Battle of Mynydd Carn, but no historian has ever found its location, and no traces of weapons or burials have been found. Maybe one day archaeological evidence will be discovered to confirm that the battle of Mynydd Carn did indeed take place on Mynydd Morfil or in one of the adjacent valleys.

Wizards and their Spirits

As indicated in Chapter 6 and also in the novels, the Newport-Nevern area had a great reputation in the past for its wise men, who served as seers or soothsayers, quack doctors, herbalists and even private investigators. They were also called conjurors, wizards or magicians, but they were definitely not in the business of performing party tricks! In Welsh, a magician would always be referred to as *dyn hysbys* or "knowing one" on the basis that he could foresee the future and look back into the past; and it was natural that ordinary people would believe him to be in touch with the spirit or supernatural world. Such men were always believed to have great leather-bound "magic books" full of charms, spells and incantations. Some were even believed to say "abracadabra" on appropriate occasions,

and to be in possession of magic wands. Indeed, when Joseph Harries dies in *Rebecca and the Angels* he does indeed turn out to possess all sorts of interesting equipment.

It was widely believed that wizards could "call down" spirits of all shapes and sizes and that they were quite safe so long as they remained within a magic circle. Some of these spirits were reputed to be very dangerous, and even the strongest of wizards would be brought to the point of exhaustion if they had to deal with them. It was also assumed that if anybody other than a wizard should seek to invoke these spirits, they might not know how to get rid of them again, and that could lead to all sorts of trouble.

A popular caricature of a wizard at work, with his accessories around him. In Wales the wizards were rather different!

Magicians were held in great esteem as scientists and men of learning, and because they underwent long periods of training we can see them as the inheritors of the Welsh druidic tradition. They were not viewed as religious figures, and indeed they were themselves not opposed to churches or church-going. But in the days of the nonconformist revivals it was perhaps natural that churchmen should denounce them as being "in league with the devil" -- and as scientific knowledge increased it was inevitable that their influence gradually declined.

The most famous magician from the local area was our friend Dr Joseph Harries of Werndew, Dinas, who is often confused with Dr John Harries, another famous magician from Cwrt-y-Cadno in Carmarthenshire. In my imagination he is the man to whom Shemi goes for his training in esoteric matters. There are many stories in the literature about his prowess in removing curses, finding lost animals, solving mysteries, and healing sick people. In the late eighteenth century John Jenkin (Ioan Siencyn), the famous schoolmaster and poet of Nevern, was reputed to be a magician or conjuror, and there are a number of very strange tales about his achievements.

Joseph Harries Werndew with his big book, in the herb garden. Well, he MIGHT have looked something like this......

Then there was Levi Salmon of Cilgwyn, known locally as "Dr Cwac", who lived at Plas y Ffynnon near Temple Bar and who was reputed to communicate with demons and to have special powers over animals. In more recent times there have been at least two other "knowing ones" in the Newport-Nevern area. One was an old man who claimed that he could talk to animals of all sorts and get them to do his bidding, and some of the locals were quite frightened in case he cast a spell over them. There is another whose family has always had a reputation for second sight, charms and spells, and it would not be a very good idea to upset any of them........

.... *and on the subject of encounters with the supernatural, let's not forget that Pentre Ifan was renowned, in the nineteenth century, as a place where fairies could be seen dancing on moonlit nights.*

10. Folk Beliefs and Traditions

When I started writing the life history of Martha Morgan, it was obvious to me that I would have to incorporate into her story occasional episodes based upon the folk traditions and beliefs of the day. Even today, every rural community has folk traditions, and they provide the cement which holds the fabric of society together. These traditions may include an annual church fete, a midnight mass at Christmas, and something jolly on the village green on May Day. The frequency of these "folk events" has certainly declined, and fewer and fewer people are involved in them, except perhaps in areas where they have been incorporated into packages designed to promote tourism; but in 1800 they were hugely important for providing opportunities for relaxation and even play, for dividing the year into segments, and for demonstrating social cohesion. In Martha's story the brief descriptions of beliefs and traditions which occur here and there in her diaries allow me, as an author, to bring in quiet episodes and to vary the pace of story and character development. At the same time these descriptions are just as important as the descriptions of landscape and weather in fixing the Saga into a particular place and time. Nowhere else, other than in this little corner of North Pembrokeshire, would anybody have encountered precisely the same mixture of jovial, eccentric and downright bizarre events..........

Ceffyl Pren

The *ceffyl pren* was strictly a "wooden horse" but was in most cases a ladder or frame used for the transport and humiliation of a person around the district so as to expose him for some great sin or disgraceful act. The tradition is said to have been derived from an ancient Welsh law abolished during Tudor times. Punished wrongdoers were generally those whose misconduct offended the strong rural sense of morality and justice: wife beaters, adulterers, young men refusing to marry girls made pregnant by them, or else neglecting to support their illegitimate children. The punishment was also much used during the Rebecca Riots on informants and tollgate keepers, and I have built the *ceffyl pren* into several sections of Martha's story.

The *ceffyl pren* tradition was widespread throughout West Wales in the early part of the 19th century. In part it was a reflection of the inadequacy of the formal justice system of the day, and in part it reflected the desire which exists in all communities for good behaviour to be maintained. So in a sense it upheld the civil law, and left the enforcement of the criminal law to the Petty Sessions and other courts. The phrase "kangaroo court" might be appropriate, since the person charged with an offence had little opportunity to defend himself; but some formalities were followed by each self-selecting jury of good men and true who carried with them the *ceffyl pren*, captured the offender and then dispensed other punishment if necessary. Sometimes that punishment would involve the use of the ducking stool.

One of the key features of the *ceffyl pren* ceremonial was that the men of the jury would always be disguised, using women's clothes and blackened faces. Since their operations were strictly outside the law there was a good deal of secrecy involved, and they often worked at night, carrying flaming torches. If there were no constables around to cause concern, they might also operate during daylight hours. In some towns and villages there would be a regular foreman of the jury, and elsewhere the foreman might be elected on the date chosen for some public humiliation. The trial and punishment of a captured offender would generally be accompanied by a mock trial and by music and laughter. So there is no doubt that entertainment as well as justice was a feature of *ceffyl pren* operations. But sometimes things got out of hand, especially if the men who made up the jury had been drinking beforehand, or if the offender decided to resist arrest. In 1844 one poor fellow was killed in Llanbadarn Trefegwys when he foolishly tried to resist those who sought to parade him around the parish for beating his wife.

Historians agree that the traditions of the *ceffyl pren* were incorporated into the Rebecca Riots, for many observers of the time noted that music and good humour, women's clothes and blackened faces, and charades and "pantomime performances" were common to both. And in both, deep beneath the frothy surface, there was a serious and steadfast intent.

Cnapan

An artist's impression of how the game might have been played. Not even the stallholders were safe!

Traditions

The ancient game of *Cnapan*, which features over and again in the pages of the Saga, has fascinated local historians, and students of the history of sport, for many generations. It has a strong claim to being the real precursor of rugby union football, although in some respects it seems to have been more akin to modern American football. George Owen, whose delightful description of *Cnapan* is justly famous, believed the game to have been invented by the Trojans or ancient Britons. This speculation is not as unreliable as we might think. Indeed, it is known that the Romans played a ball game called *Harpastum* which involved both carrying and scrummaging, and they also invented a game called *Soule* which survived in Brittany until 1870. It is therefore not beyond the bounds of possibility that the origins of *Cnapan* go back 2,000 years or more.

Where did the name come from? In North Pembrokeshire Welsh dialect the word "*cnap*" meant a lump. In the 1800's the word "*cnappan*" was used in south Cardiganshire as a verb meaning "to knock" or "to hammer away at" a person; and in Cilgerran a small section of the cliff on the edge of the Teifi gorge is known locally to this day as Gardd-y-Cnappan. *Cnapan* was the word given to the ball used in the game; it was made of solid wood, and was somwhat larger than a cricket ball. And just to make things interesting, it was boiled in tallow in order to make it slippery and difficult to hold! The object of the game was to smuggle or throw the *cnapan*, by one means or another, to the opposition "goal". In the cross-country games this goal might be the porch of the parish church, and in games on the beach it might be a wooden post stuck into the sand. The labourers played on foot, and the gentry used horses; and that must have created many extremely dangerous situations. The foot players were allowed no implements or weapons, but the gentry were allowed to use cudgels or sticks, no doubt intended for striking the ball but actually used for striking opponents instead! On the great "*Cnapan Days*" there might be a thousand players on each side.

Clearly the game was both popular and widely played in Elizabethan North Pembrokeshire, and it was a famous spectator sport as well. The main matches were occasions for huge gatherings of local people and for merchants, pedlars, and traders from far and wide who would assemble to sell food, drink and other wares. They were also social occasions for the local gentry, who would turn up both to see and be seen. There was a lot of gambling. And just as modern football managers share in the glory of their successful teams, the local gentry who acted as

The cnapan ball which was at one time kept in the Carmarthen County Museum. It is reputed to have come from Cilgerran

matchmakers saw *Cnapan* games as important occasions for enhancing both their sporting reputations and their social status.

By the late eighteenth century the game of *Cnapan* was being played in a somewhat debased form. There were worries about the increasing violence of the game and the lack of respect among players for its written or unwritten rules. The use of staves and cudgels and the involvement of horsemen among the foot-players must have led to frequent injuries. And the sight of broken limbs and bloodied bodies on *Cnapan Days* must have caused considerable concern. Henry Vlll had attempted to ban the game in Tudor times, and now the clamour for it to be declared unlawful increased. But it was none too easy to prohibit traditional games in the remote rural districts, especially those which were played on the great holiday or feast days. After all, those who worked on the land had only six or seven days during the year on which they could really enjoy themselves. So the decline and fall of *Cnapan* was probably related not so much to new legislation or safety concerns as to changing farming practices. Over a long period of time the ancient North Pembrokeshire landscape of open farmed fields and extensive common lands was transformed by the process of enclosure. Landowners built hedges, walls and fences in order to demarcate their territory, to provide shelter and to contain their stock. As pointed out in Chapter 7, many of the common lands were illegally gobbled up in the process, and the losers were the smallholders and peasant farmers who had depended on these lands for grazing their animals. Another loser was the game of *Cnapan*. Whereas it had previously been played across miles of open countryside, the game could now only take place on sandy beaches such as Traeth Mawr, Newport, or on smaller open spaces owned by members of the gentry who had sporting inclinations. Under this inexorable pressure, the game was eventually killed off in North Pembrokeshire. With the aid of a few colleagues I tried to restart the game (without the horsemen and the cudgels!) in 1985 with an annual contest between Newport and Nevern. We had a lot of fun for ten years, but then we had to abandon the game because we could not obtain insurance cover.

In each team there were three sorts of players: *"Of the first part there shall be sturdy gamesmen who shall remain in the throng or main body of the game. Of the second part there shall be scouts or fore-runners who shall be exceeding fleet of foot and who shall always strive to keep before the cnapan. Of the third part there shall be borderers who shall remain at the edges of the play. These borderers shall seek by surreption to snatch the cnapan from the contrary party, and shall hinder those who break from the body of the game and who would transport the cnapan towards the cnapan post. It is said that the gamesmen of the main throng shall be men of strength in disputing, boldness in assaulting, and stoutness in resisting; the scouts or forerunners shall be lusty hurlers of the cnapan and also men of agility and good footmanship, able to fly swift as an arrow and be able to show skilful deliverance of the cnapan to those that be with them; and the borderers shall with wondrous invention prevent those who run against them, leaping upon them without fear to take them out of the game."*

There were great scrummages involving the "sturdy gamesmen" or forwards, and if the game was stopped for any reason it was restarted by throwing the ball high into the air so that it could be caught by a man leaping high. No kicking of the ball was possible, so this game was not like the primitive "street football" contests that occurred in many parts of the British Isles. But there were so many similarities with modern rugby football that Newport in Pembrokeshire lays a good claim (better than Rugby School, at any rate) to be the place where rugby really began.

In the Saga I have based my descriptions of the game, and of what went on around the edges of it, quite closely on George Owen's old account. I knew right from the beginning that David's violent death would have to take place on Traeth Mawr, at the water's edge, at a time when Martha, and the reader, might least expect such a tragedy.

Mari Lwyd

The *Mari Lwyd* ceremony is described in House of Angels, and it is invested with much significance by Martha and her family. And a strange ceremony it is. *Mari Lwyd* (Grey Mare / Holy Mary) was the name most generally applied in Wales to the horse-figure formerly carried from door to door by wassail-singing groups during the Christmas season. This figure (which is, of course, also represented in other countries) seems to have been once known all over southern Wales, but the detail varied from one county to another. The attendant ritual began with the singing of traditional stanzas by the *Mari Lwyd* group at the door, soliciting both permission to sing and enter into the house, and issuing a challenge to a versifying contest. In some areas this was followed by the *pwnco*, a debate or contest conducted to the same music in a combination of traditional and impromptu stanzas, between a member of the group and an opponent within the house. This usually amounted to heavy leg-pulling in which the contestants mocked each other's singing, drunkenness, lack of generosity, and so forth.

Victory in the debate for the *Mari Lwyd* group (which was of course inevitable) would ensure admission into the house, to partake of cakes and ale and perhaps collect a money gift as well. In at least some cases, after the end of the debate, the group would sing additional stanzas introducing its individual members and finally, after entertaining the occupants of the house, it would deliver a farewell song.

When Martha and her children are visited by the strange horse-like monster and its attendants, she is very touched, and recognizes that it is a sign from the community that she is not only accepted but also loved by a great many people.

Plygain

The Christmas tradition of *Plygain* goes back hundreds of years. In the last century it was very common for people in the country districts to stay up all night on Christmas Eve in order to attend the

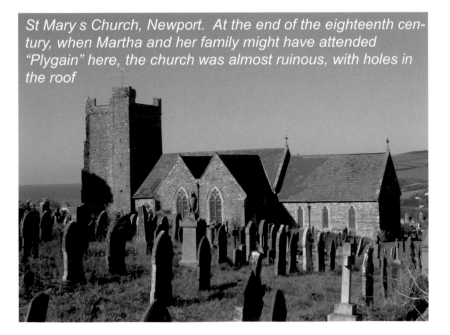

St Mary s Church, Newport. At the end of the eighteenth century, when Martha and her family might have attended "Plygain" here, the church was almost ruinous, with holes in the roof

Plygain service in the parish church at 3 am (or, more commonly, 6 am) before dawn on Christmas Morning. It would end when the first glimmers of dawn appeared in the east. The service was in some places a prayer meeting, but more commonly it was a service devoted to the unaccompanied singing of special hymns written in the traditional Welsh metres and sung to old tunes. Another part of the tradition was the carrying of candles to symbolize the coming of the Light of the World; and this tradition may indeed be pre-Christian, with torches or candle-light used to signal the turning of the year and the return of longer days and shorter nights.

Newport is one of the few places in Wales where the *Plygain* service still survives, attended by people of all denominations, and held in the Church Chapel at the top of Upper St Mary Street. The ecumenical nature of the service is interesting, since the Church Chapel (which is now used as a church hall) was used by the Methodists from 1799 until they seceded from the established church in 1811. The service is, as always, conducted entirely in Welsh. When Martha attends the *Plygain* for the first time, she is entranced by the beauty of the glittering procession of worshippers on their way to the church, but she is not so entranced by the length of the service itself!

The Ducking Stool

The Newport ducking-stool, located on the estuary, is used on occasion in the Saga in the punishment of offenders, following "sentencing" from the jury of the *Ceffyl Pren*. It was generally a strongly made wooden chair (the surviving specimens are of oak) in which the culprit was seated, an iron band being placed around him so that he should not fall out during immersion. Usually the chair was fastened to a long wooden beam fixed as a seesaw on the edge of a pond or river. Sometimes, however, the ducking-stool was not a fixture but was mounted on a pair of wooden wheels so that it could be moved through the streets, and at the river-edge was hung by a

The Newport ducking stool would have been used on the Parrog, or inside the reclaimed area on the edge of the marsh

chain from the end of a beam. The guilty person would then be ducked a specified number of times, with total immersion if the water was deep enough. In some areas the ducking stool was used following formal sentencing by the magistrates, and it was reserved for females found guilty of witchcraft or other crimes. Sometimes the punishment proved fatal for elderly women, if they were immersed too frequently or too deeply.

Hen Galan

As indicated in Chapter 4, every year those who live in Cwm Gwaun celebrate New Year not once but twice, thanks to a tradition which

dates back to the middle of the eighteenth century. *Hen Galan* literally means "Old beginning of the month", and the tradition arises
from the decision in 1752 to change from the old Julian calendar to
the newer Gregorian calendar which was more accurate. Thirteen
days were "lost" in the process, as a result of which there were protests across the kingdom from those who believed that they would
be be paid less by their employers or even that their lives had suddenly been shortened. Things gradually settled down across the rest
of the country, but in Cwm Gwaun, the valley families were so attached to the Old New Year that they continued to celebrate it on
13th January. The tradition continues to this day.

Until quite recently it was the tradition for the children of the
valley schools to have the day off for *Hen Galan*, and they would
travel about from house to house giving imprompu performances of
a special carol and begging for *calennig*. They would be rewarded
with gifts of fruit, sweets or money. But the main feature of *Hen
Galan*, as far as adults are concerned, is the opportunity to meet up
with friends and families during the evening. So there are parties all

*Cwm Gwaun, not far from Pontfaen,
where Hen Galan is still celebrated*

over the valley, with long traditions of hospitality kept alive. In Martha's diaries she makes it clear that every year, at *Hen Galan*, the Morgan family of Plas Ingli pays a social visit to the Laugharne family of Plas Pontfaen. That is the tradition, and it is respected except in the most exceptional of circumstances. That sort of thing would have been typical in 1797 from one end of the valley to the other.

Christmas and New Year

The traditions associated with Christmas and New Year were probably the most important of all in the rural community of North Pembrokeshire. It was the only opportunity that people of all classes had for relaxation and feasting over a period of at least a week. True, animals still had to be fed and watered, eggs had to be collected, and cows had to be milked, but at that time of uncertain winter weather it was possible to leave the fields to themselves for a few days without worrying too much about to the consequences.

So this was the time for the gentry to demonstrate their generosity to friends, neighbours, tenants, and labourers and their families, and thereby to enhance their reputations. Of course, that generosity would vary from year to year depending upon the success or failure of the previous year's harvesting and trading activities. As I have tried to demonstrate in the pages of Martha's diaries, there were fat years and lean years, and if things were desperate financially Christmas would almost literally be cancelled. It also happened that if there was a death in a gentry family, or some other tragedy, that family would not be expected to lay on lavish feasts and other ceremonials for the sake of others. On such occasions some of the less affluent families of the neighbourhood would organize Christmas on a less lavish scale, thereby spreading the load.

But if times were good, much was expected of a squire and mistress of a respectable estate, and everybody involved could look forward to the festive season for many weeks. The necessary advance planning tested the skill and resolve of even the most efficient housekeeper, and the quantities of food and drink required were impressive indeed. I have tried to indicate this in the descriptions of the festive season in various parts of Martha's story. The catering details varied from one estate to another, but I have built into the Plas Ingli Christmas just some of the conventions gleaned from contemporary descriptions from real gentry houses.

There is no point in repeating the detail here, but we must also note that Christmas and New Year were the times when complicated payments and repayments came into play between landlord and tenant, master and servant, and even between the members of extended families. As explained in the pages of the novels, there was little cash moving about in the North Pembrokeshire farming community, and "in kind" payments were routine instead of (or as part of) rental payments. So at Christmas time geese, ducks, eggs, chickens, butter, cheese, and all sorts of other products would be contributed by labourers and tenants to the mountain of food being assembled by the housekeeper of a well-run estate. And the hospitality provided by the host and hostess was not simply a matter of benevolence either, for they paid very little in the way of wages to those who worked for them. The Christmas extravaganza was actually owed to servants, labours and tenants in exchange for their loyalty and hard work during the course of the year that was now coming to an end. The Christmas feast, wildly excessive though it often was, was actually present in every unwritten contract, and everybody knew it.

Harvest -- the Wrach

In rural communities across Europe there are -- or were -- traditions, some of them apparently pagan in origin, associated with the successful completion of the harvest. In many traditions the last piece of corn to be cut was the focus of attention. In Wales, this was plaited while still standing, and was called the witch or *wrach*. Great was the excitement among the reapers when the last patch of standing

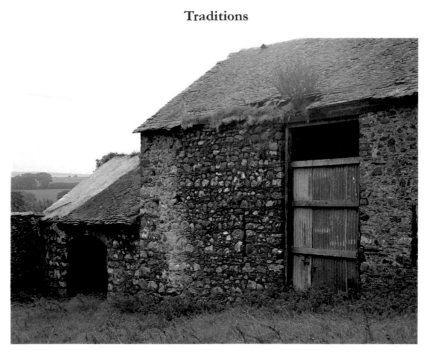

An old barn not far from Fishguard. Note the large door, needed for threshing and winnowing. Barns such as this were crucial for the good storage of barley in particular

corn was reached. All in turn threw their sickles at it, and the one who succeeded in cutting it received a jug of home-brewed ale or some other reward such as a kiss from all of the females present. In Pembrokeshire the *wrach* was then carried home by the winning reaper, followed by the other reapers, who tried to snatch her away. If the man carrying her got her safely to the big house, it would be kept in a prominent position until replaced by the *wrach* from the next harvest. If the reaping was on a tenant farm, the farmer kept her in his kitchen till the following year and, on the day of the first spring ploughing, took whatever grain remained intact on her and fed it to his horses or mixed it with the seed to be sown to ensure fertility.

In the tenant farming community there was another tradition. Sometimes the first *wrach* to be made would be rushed off to a neighbouring farm, where the reapers might still be busy at their work. But the bearer had to be very careful not to be observed by his neighbours, for if they saw him coming and had the least suspicion of his errand they would force him away again. So, creeping stealthily up behind a hedge he would wait till the foreman of his neighbour's reapers was just opposite him and within easy reach. Then he would throw the *wrach* over the fence and, if possible, upon the foreman's sickle. He would take to his heels and make off as fast as he could run, and he was a lucky man if he escaped without being caught or cut by the flying sickles which the infuriated reapers hurled after him. Was that all just horseplay and friendly rivalry between neighbouring farms? Or was there some deeper significance to it, dating back to the Iron Age when there actually was mayhem and even warfare at harvest time? In the learned tomes about folk traditions there are plenty of explanations, some more plausible than others.

Other Oddities

There are many other traditions and folk beliefs which pop up in the pages of Martha's diaries, including the Green Man tradition, the *twmpath*, the hunting of squirrels at Christmas time, the *rhamanta* or divination ceremony, the ceremony of the Easter water, the *pwnc* which occurred in many chapels, the placing of the plough under the kitchen table, and the traditions associated with funerals and burials.

These -- and a multitude of others -- are referred to in the texts by Trefor Owen and Gwynn Jones which are included in the list at the end of the book; but for me to deal with them in any detail I would have to write another book!

11. Full Character List

There are more than 200 characters who play major and minor roles in the saga. Some of them have proved to be mischievous, and have ended up in the wrong places at the wrong times! I have tried to put right all inconsistencies in reprints and in the later books of the series. In particular, I realized that in the first edition of *On Angel Mountain* Martha's father was given the name of George Howell, which was the same name as one of the dastardly squires who plots Martha's downfall. So he was renamed Charles Tudor for the Corgi edition of the book. This means that Martha's maiden name was also Tudor, giving just a hint of royal blood! The other name change which some readers might have noticed is that of Dai Darjeeling the tea merchant. I discovered that all the tea coming into Britain at the time of these stories came from China, and not India, and this led to him being renamed Dai Canton in the Corgi editions!

The Morgan family of Plas Ingli

Grandpa Isaac Morgan, born 1740, married in Jan 1758, died 1820
    (two children, William born 1758 and Betty born 1760)
Grandma Jane, born 1742, married 1758, died 1821
William (David's father), b Dec 1758, married 1776, died in fire 1794
Bethan (David's mother), b 1760, married 1776, died in fire 1794
Griffith (David's brother), b 1776, lost at sea 1796
David, born 10 June 1777. Married Martha Howell on 21 Aug 1796.
    Died 12 Feb 1805, aged 27
Thomas (small brother) born 1781, died in fire 1794
George (small brother) b 1785, died in fire 1794
Rose (small sister) born 1790, died in fire 1794
Betty (David's aunt) born 1760, resident in Solva, d 1830

The Howell (Tudor) family of Brawdy

Charles Howell (Martha's father) born 1745, married 1765, died Dec 1817. (Renamed as Tudor in Corgi edition)

Betsi (Martha's mother), born 1748, married 1765, died 1841, aged 93.

Sioned and Sion (twins born 1767, died in infancy 1768)

Morys (older brother) born 1770, Baptist minister in Haverfordwest, married Nansi 1797. Three children, Edward, b 1799 (wife Susan), Jane, b 1802, Robert, b 1805. Took over Brawdy estate 1817. Died 1845.

Elen, oldest sister, born 1773, "married to her music" in Bristol. Illegitimate son Brynach b 7 April 1807. Emigrated to USA 1807, m Tom Bradshaw 1810. Two other children, Susanna b 1812 and George b 1815.

Catrin, sister born 1776, moved to Castlebythe as tutor 1797. Married James Bowen in 1800. Two children, John, b 1803, Mark, b 1806.

Martha, born 12 May 1778 at Brawdy. Married to David on 21 August 1796. Died 27 Feb 1855, aged 76.

The children of David and Martha

Betsi, born March 22, 1798; married Ioan Rhys of Cenarth in 1818. Son Benjamin, b 18 Sept, 1821 (m Sally-Anne Mortimer of Stone Hall 1848, son Joshua b 1851), son Abel, b 1823 (m Susan 1847, daughter Jane, b 1850), son Owain, b 14 Jan 1829.

Daisy, born April 10, 1801; off to London 1821 and in with Regency set. Married George Havard 1846 and moved to town. Illegitimate children Amy, b 1832, John, b 1826 (m Molly 1850, daughter Anna, b 1852), William, b 1829.

Dewi, born Feb 4, 1803; drowned Jan 1820, aged 16.

Sara, born March 19, 1805; died 1830, aged 25

Brynach, born 7 April 1807 (adopted by Martha). Married Anne
      Edwards 1830. Daughter Rose, b 21 June 1831; son David, b
      15 Aug 1834. Brynach inherited Llanychaer estate from
      George Price in 1832. Anne died in childbirth 1837.

((Rose (18) married Henry Evans (23) in Caersalem Chapel 1849.
Their son Levi, b 1852. The family all moved to Pembroke Dock
1875, when Levi was 23.))

The Laugharne Family of Pontfaen

John Laugharne, Squire of Pontfaen, b 1743, m 1769, d 1810

Olwen Laugharne, his wife, b 1750, m 1769, d 1815

James (b 1773), oldest son, barrister in Carmarthen, took over estate
      1810, married Mary Vaughan of Jordanston 1811, when aged
      38. Son Thomas, b 1814, daughter Dilly, b 1820.

Mary Jane (b 1775), oldest daughter. Married Dafydd Stokes of
      Trecwn 1800. Children William b 1804, Samuel, b 1811. Great
      friend of Martha.

Liza (b 1777), younger daughter, married 1800 to Walter Allen of
      Cresselly. Unhappy marriage. No children.

Owain Laugharne, b 28 Dec 1780, youngest brother of Mary Jane.
      Took over Llannerch in 1802 following purchase by his
      father. Missing for 15 yrs. Died Feb 1825.

The Price Family of Llanychaer

George Price, Plas Llanychaer, b. 1742, d 1832 aged 90

Susan Price, b 1748, married George 1768, d 1817 aged 67

Herbert, son b 1769, should have inherited the estate but d 1803

Iestyn, son b 1771, joined the Royal Horse Artillery 1796, invalided out (presumed dead) 1807, died 1822. Son Brynach, born illegitimately 7 April 1807

Susanna, oldest daughter, b 1772, m John Warlow 1794, moved to Carms. Widowed 1802. Illegitimate son Ethan, b May 1807.

Mary, daughter, b 1775, m 1795, moved to Merthyr Tydfil.

Fanny, daughter b 1786, living at home 1808. Suicide 1817.

Plas Ingli Staff

Bessie Walter, born Bessie Gruffydd in 1776. Maid. Started at the Plas in 1795. Left to marry Benji Walter in 1799. Moved back to the Plas after death of husband and son 1802. Housekeeper from 1812. Died 1857, aged 81.

Billy Ifans, born 1763. Carter and senior man. Started at the Plas when he was 14. Died 1823.

Gomer Jenkins, b 1812, started at the Plas 1827. Son of Shemi and Sian. Married Gwenno 1840. Tenancy at Penrhiw after 1844.

Shemi Jenkins, born 1782. Gardener and farm labourer. Started work 1797. From Blaenwaun, oldest son of Daniel Jenkins. Married 1810 to Sian. Left to be a wizard 1836.

Hettie Jones, dairymaid 1797. In 1805-6 helped now and then.

Moses Lloyd, b 1773, youngest son of old Squire Lloyd of Cwmgloyn, brother to Meredith and Matthew. Labourer and gardener, started at the Plas 1793. Killed by Martha in self-defence 1797.

Blodwen Owen, born 1750. Housekeeper/cook (widowed -- four children: Bethan, Sian, Dafydd, Will). Started at the Plas 1765. Retired ill 1812, died 1814.

Will Owen, Mrs Owens' son, b 1780, shepherd and cow-man after 1806. Married Tegwen Gruffydd 1823, and moved into estate cottage. Three children, Gerallt, b 1824, Myfanwy, b 1828, Bronwen, b 1831. Head man 1836. Moved back to the Plas after death of Tegwen in 1850

Character List

Myfanwy Owen, b 1828, started at the Plas 1845 as dairy-maid.

Gerallt Owen, b 1824, started at the Plas 1845 as cow-man.

Gwenno Philpin, housemaid, b 1810, started in service 1827.
Married Gomer Jenkins 1840. At Penrhiw 1844. Part-time
dairymaid 1845. Son Gwyn and daughter Gwenllan (twins) b
on Christmas Day 1845. Other children Robert, b 1848 and
Jenny, b 1850.

Liza Philpin, wet nurse, b 1784, from Pantry. Married Tomos 1806,
when aged 22. Two children, Twm (b 1807, d 1822) and
Gwenno, b 1810. Housemaid from 1814. Later Martha's
"lady's maid". Died 1845.

Bryn Williams, b 1803. Cousin of Will. From Dinas. Worked in
Merthyr Tydfil, involved in insurrection 1831. Servant from
1833. Died 1843.

Sian Williams, b 1779, daughter of Caradoc and Bethan Williams of
Gelli, taken on as nursemaid in 1798. Married Shemi 1810.
Three children John, b 1811, Gomer, b 1812, Molly, b 1816.
From 1845 housekeeper for Capt Davids in Dinas.

Blodwen Bebb, b illegitimately 1797, started at the Plas 1845 as
dairy-maid.

Other Characters

Levi Abbs and wife Maggie, labourer, Penrhiw Fach.

Skiff Abraham, b 1782, small-time criminal and friend of Will Owen,
Abby, Faggot, Halfpint and Daffy. Married Maria 1812, three
children, Rhiannon, b 1814, Josie, b 1816 and Annie, b 1820.
Wealthy merchant and smuggling supremo in 1846.

John Bateman, Martha's tutor 1805 and steward of Pontfaen estate.
Died 1821.

Byron Bailes, Squire of Puncheston. Good old fellow.

Rosie Bebb, poor girl on Long Street. Child Blodwen fathered by
Matthew Lloyd, b 1797.

Character List

Ifan Beynon of Berry Hill. Was clerk to the Justices; jailed 1797 and released 1801 after 4 years hard labour. Executed Feb 1807.

Maldwyn Biggs, local thug from Newport. Hired to sabotage Owain's boat. Died 1817.

George Billings, Post-goch, tenant on Bayvil estate 1837.

Mary Billings, lodging-house keeper on the Parrog 1800.

Eleanor (Ellie) Bowen, born 1776, oldest daughter of the Squire of Llwyngwair. Martha's friend. Married Walter Phillips of Ambleston in 1808, Children: Jasper, b 1810, Margaret, b 1812, John, b 1815. Unhappy marriage. Died 1851.

John Bowen, squire of Llwyngwair, senior JP, father to Ellie and William. Died 1810.

William Bowen, squire of Llwyngwair after 1810. Ellie's brother. B 1770, m Jane 1800, d 1855.

Thomas Bullin, toll-farmer working under contract to the Turnpike Trusts 1839-44.

Benjamin Bullin, brother of Thomas, gatekeeper at Efailwen 1839.

John Campbell, Baron Cawdor (father), the most powerful squire in Pembs,d 1821.

John Frederick Campbell (son), Earl Cawdor, b 1790, succeeded to Stackpole Estate 1821.

Billy Clog, cobbler from Newport 1800.

Freddy Cobb, local thug from Parrog, worked once at Havard's shipyard. Sabotaged Owain's boat. Died 1817.

Morgan Cobb, lived on Parrog next door to Davy Death in 1806.

Arwel Coggs, one of Eynon's spies 1843.

Cynog Cole, Candle Maker, Newport. Mrs Owen had her eye on him in 1800.

Elijah Collins, Llysmeddyg, old merchant from Newport. B 1750. Friend of Grandpa. D 1846, aged 96. Helps Martha.

Seamus Collins, cousin of Elijah, in Ireland 1854.

John Collyer, b 1770, one-time suitor to Martha (1806), heir to Tredafydd estate. Kindly fellow. Married 1809, son Justin, b 1812. Died 1849.

Ifan Dafis Drover, cattle dealer from Eglwyswrw.

Character List

William Daniels, Clerk to the Justices 1806. Coroner 1846-55.

Dominic Cunningham, b 1810, servant at Wiston Mill, from Co Clare
(real name Patrick O'Grady).

Dai Darjeeling, tea merchant. B 1766. In love with Bessie. Died
1846. (Renamed Dai Canton in Transworld editions.)

Eli Davids, sailor hired by Moses Lloyd to kill David's brother
Griffith in 1796. Died 1797.

Saul Davids, sea captain, b 1880, from Dinas (Sian worked for him
1845). Good man.

David Davies (Dai'r Cantwr). Member of the "Stag and Pheasant"
gang, executed for murder 1845. Villain in Rebecca Riots.

Davy Davies (Davy Death), carpenter / undertaker / chandler,
b 1766, d 1852, aged 86.

Lloyd Davies, Glynsaithmaen farmer. B 1785. Distant cousin of Will.
Friend to Martha. Involved in Rebecca Riots.

Jane Davis, old woman on the Parrog 1838.

Dafydd Deliverance, postman 1854.

John Devonald, Rector of Newport, mostly absentee. Retired 1825.

John Dickins, Revenue Officer from Milford Haven.

Jenkin Edwards of Llwyngoras, b 1725, old squire and justice, friend
of Grandpa, purchased Henllys 1798. Died 1810.

Martin Edwards of Llwyngoras, son of Jenkin, b 1760, d 1832.

Solomon Edwards of Llwyngoras, son of Martin, b 1795, died 1866.

Anne Edwards Trefach, b 5 Jan 1807, 3rd daughter of Rhys, girl
friend of Brynach in 1822, m 1830, died in childbirth 1837.

Rhys Edwards of Trefach, b 1766, son of William. Good man,
m Bronwen 1788, d 1850. Children Amelia, b 1790, Jane, b
1799, Anne, b 1807.

William Edwards of Trefach, tutor to Martha, b 1733, d 1809.

Thomas Elias of London, fraudulently worked as an attorney until
jailed in 1797. Let out 1805 after 8 years hard labour.
Transported 1807.

Patty Ellis (Nicholas), prostitute living on the Parrog, b 1776.
Married Jake in March 1807. Daughter Mary, b Feb 1808, son
Jack, b 1810, son Hubert, b 1813, daughter Amy, b 1816.

Character List

Evan Evans, Newport, temporary and reluctant constable 1806.

Henry Evans, b 1826, son of Capt Billy Evans, sea captain from the
    Parrog. Married Rose 1849. Son Levi, b 1852.

Nathaniel Evans, Waunbayvil, tenant on Bayvil estate 1837.
    Murdered by John Owen 1844. Villain in Rebecca Riots.

Henry Eynon, bailiff in 1837, Clerk to Justices 1843-44. Spymaster
    for magistrates. Murdered by Zeke and others in 1844. Villain
    in Rebecca Riots.

John Fenton of Glynymel, son of Richard Fenton. Spent much time
    in London with the "Regency set." Died in a bog Dec 1806.

Richard Fenton, Squire of Glynymel, purchased Pentre Ifan 1798, a
    good friend of Martha. Scholar and antiquarian. Died 1821.

Tom Flannel, ran the fulling mill at Pandy around 1806.

Thomas Campbell Foster, reporter for the Times, b 1813. In Pembs
    1843-44. Friend to Martha.

Jethro Gittins -- squire of Tredrissi 1800.

Mostyn Gittins (b 1780), son of Jethro, met Martha 1806. M Rose
    Jenkins 1807. Ally in 1840.

Alwyn Gittins, squire of Tredrissi 1845.

Will Gittins, wife Annie and two daughters, labourers, living at
    Trefelin 1797.

Mistress Griffin, Martha's jailer in Haverfordwest in 1797.

Gwynfor Griffith, senior constable 1846.

Aeron Griffiths, b 1773, oldest son of Gethin and Liza, took over
    Dolrannog Isaf on death of Gethin in 1835. Died 1842. Oldest
    son Jethro (b 1804) took over in 1842.

Gethin Griffiths (b 1740) and wife Liza. Married 1770. Tenant
    farmers at Dolrannog Isaf as from 1800. Good contacts in
    smuggling world. Three children, Aeron, b 1773, others 1776
    and 1780. Gethin died aged 75 in 1835.

George Griffiths (b 1716) and wife Mair (b 1720), parents of Gethin.
    In 1797 his old mother Bethan was still alive -- aged 99. Used
    to be Dolrannog Isaf tenants -- after 1800 in a tied cottage on
    the estate. Both died 1806.

Character List

Jethro Griffiths, b 1804, m 1826, d 1888. Daughter Eliza d 1844 soon after birth. Tenant from 1842..

Andrew Gruffydd, Penybont (cottage in woods), Bessie's uncle. Daughter Jenny worked at Cilgwyn Mawr 1806.

John Gruffydd, Tregroes, honest ally of Plas Ingli.

Robert Gruffydd, Nevern. Bessie's father, d 1810.

Wilmot Gwynne, b 1895, from Swansea, took over Llanychaer and Plas Ingli estates 1845. Married Delilah 1820. Son Samson, b 1822, son Joshua, b 1825, daughter Maria, b 1829.

Tomos Gwyther, Greystones, involved in French Invasion with David. Injured by the French 1797.

Lloyd Hall, attorney (in Rebecca Riots) 1839.

John Harries, wizard of Cwrt-y-Cadno, died 1839. Teacher for Shemi.

Joseph Harries of Werndew, known as "the wizard", but also inventor, herbalist, doctor, healer and sleuth, born 1761, m 1788, wife and baby died in childbirth, died 4th Feb 1826. Martha's friend and mentor.

Hubert Harry, b 1760, bad merchant from Newport. Hated by local people. Died 1840.

Jacob Harry, son, b 1792. Also a merchant in 1845.. Enemy of Martha. Died 1854 (lynched in Ireland).

Stephen Havard, shipbuilder on the estuary in 1800. Brother of Havard Medical

William Havard Medical. Only qualified doctor / surgeon in Newport. Died 1823.

George Havard Medical. Son of William -- b 1790, took over as doctor 1822. Married Daisy 1846.

Griff Hickey, excise man from Fishguard 1806.. Covered Newport area.

Mary Higgins, witch living at Allt Clydach in 1806.

Thomas Higgins, second son of Scolton Manor estate 1806. Rather stupid.

Mark Higgon, good Squire of Tredafydd, cousin of Vaughan Castlebythe. Magistrate 1843.

Character List

Morris Higgon, Trepant (near Morfil) 1797. Involved in Battle in the Sky episode.

Ifan Hipkins, corrupt doctor from Cardigan 1855.

George Howell, Squire of Henllys 1797. Wife Megan. Son John, daughter Mary. Died (suicide) 1797. Villain in the first story.

John Howell, son of George Howell. Moved to Fishguard with mother Megan and sister Mary after loss of the estate. Joined the army in 1799. Executed Feb 1807. Villain in second story.

William Howell, illegitimate son of John Howell, b 1805, A spy during Rebecca Riots 1840. Merchant in 1845. Steward of Barony 1854. Murdered 1854.

Morris Hughes, Steward of the Barony of Cemaes 1806.

James Humfrey, servant at Tredrissi (Gittins estate) in 1826.

Solomon Huws, Bayvil, bad squire, died aged 70 in 1823.

Arfon and Delyth Huws, labourers on Tredrissi estate 1826.

Madoc Huws, b 1780, took over Bayvil estate 1823, enemy of Martha in 1843. Murdered 1855.

Tomos Huws and wife Myfanwy and family, Plain Dealings, labourer 1797.

Dafydd Ifan, Gamallt, leader of *Ceffyl Pren* mob 1837. Once a tenant of Martha. Involved in Rebecca Riots.

Sion ap Ifan and Huw ap Ifan, thugs and petty criminals from Newport. Transported 1807.

Charles Ifans, farmer at Tycanol Farm 1846.

George Ifans, Tregwynt, Brynberian. Small farmer -- Amos Jones lodges with him 1845-6.

Jacob Ifans, Minister of Jabes Chapel 1824.

Mary Ifans, servant to Elijah Collins 1845.

Matthew Ifans, Eglwyswrw, and wife Lettice. Billy's parents. Good folks

Will Ifans and wife Daisy, tenants of Dolrannog Uchaf in 1800, in a tied cottage after 1806. In second story.

Shoni James, wealthy merchant from Newport. Honest man.

Abel Jenkins, Brynaeron, and wife Mari. Labourer, b 1858. Brothers are Abraham and George.

Character List

Abraham Jenkins, Brithdir Mawr, b 1756, farmer and supporter of Morgan family in 1797.

Daniel Jenkins, Blaenwaun, cottager, father of Shemi, b 1760, died 1822.

George Jenkins, b 1758, brother to Abraham and Abel. Innkeeper at Penybont in 1797.

Simeon Jenkins, son and heir of Cilciffeth estate 1806. Arrogant and silly fellow.

John Jeremy, teacher in Mistress Bowen's Circulating School 1808.

James Jobbins, Squire of Holmws, magistrate 1837. Enemy of Martha in 1843. Murdered 1855.

Jacob Jobbins, senior deacon of Capel Brynberian in 1846.

Herbert Johns (Herbert Herbal), green man 1830.

Caleb and Annie Jones, Siop Fach, Newport.

Amos Jones (Jones Minor Prophet) b 1785, m 1808 to Hannah (d 1846) and lived in Radnor. No children. Old mother in Brecon d 1846. Murdered 12 Feb 1855.

Hettie Jones, born 1770. Three surviving children. Worked at the Plas as dairymaid from 1795. Left to start her own lodging house 1802. Husband lost at sea 1801. Died 1835.

Jacob Jones, b 1875. Elderly spy working for Martha 1843.

John Jones (Shoni Sgubor Fawr) Leader of the Stag and Pheasant gang, executed for murder 1845. Villain in Rebecca Riots.

Thomas Jones, senior deacon of Capel Brynberian in 1846.

Zeke Jones, son of Hettie, b 1800. Ally of Martha 1840-43.

John Ladd, Mayor of Newport 1797 and 1805.

Dafydd Laugharne, Squire of Pengelli Fawr 1845-55. Also a magistrate. Villain in final book. Executed 1855.

Rees Laugharne, Pengelli Fawr, bad squire in 1800. Younger son Dafydd is Squire 1845-1855.

George Lewis (Lewis Legal). Family lawyer from Fishguard, b 1740, d 1828.

Hywel Lewis, Trecenydd, tenant on Bayvil estate 1837.

Ianto Llewelyn, drover, owed Martha £800. At Garnmeini 1849.

Character List

Matthew Lloyd, b 1772, brother of Meredith and Moses, who died 1797. Married 1804, one child b 1805, cottage on Cwmgloyn estate. Executed Feb 1807. Villain in second book.

Meredith Lloyd, b 1770, wife Jane, 2 small children, took over as Squire of Cwmgloyn on death of old squire in 1805. Children are Nicholas, b 1797 and Mabel, b 1800. Died 1833.

Moses Lloyd, b 1773, disinherited by his father, the old Squire of Cwmgloyn. Worked as a servant at the Plas before the fire and afterwards. Sent packing from the Plas in March 1797. Killed in the confrontation with Martha in the cave on 23 Aug 1797.

Nicholas Lloyd, son of Meredith, b 1797, m 1820, took over as squire 1833. Ally of Martha. Died young, in 1844.

Joshua Lloyd, oldest son of Nicholas, b 1821, squire of Cwmgloyn from 1844. Ally of Martha in last book.

Thomas Lloyd, Lord Marcher 1847 - 1855. Lived in Carmarthen since castle was ruinous.

Stephen Lloyd, senior deacon of Capel Brynberian in 1846.

Richard Lord, steward of Bayvil estate 1837, later Clerk to the Justices (1843).

James Frederick Love, Colonel, commander of Military Operations in Wales 1843-44, during Rebecca Riots.

Benjamin Mathias, cobbler, Newport. Constable 1797.

Bethan Mathias, Cilwen, b 1786, teacher for Betsi.

George Mathias, Trehaidd. Wife Ellen was Will's cousin. Radical sympathiser 1839.

Gwilym Mathias, b 1788, brother of Bethan, Cilwen. (Father Eli died in fire 1794). Ally in 1840.

Thomas Mathias, Mayor 1803.

Alexander Milton, corn merchant from Fishguard. Bought Plas Ingli barley 1797

Abel Morgan, sea captain from Parrog 1800.

William Morgan, tenant at Llannerch after disappearance of Owain in 1807.

Bobby Morris, b 1812, in love with Gwenno 1832. Died 1843. Villain in Rebecca Riots.

Character List

Luke Morris, sea captain living on Parrog.

Robert Morris Legal, solicitor from Fishguard 1843-44.

Jake Nicholas, sailor in love with Patty Ellis. B 1780. Married to Patty 25 March 1807. By 1822, owned 4 fishing smacks. Four children. Successful merchant 1846-55.

Jack Nicholas, son to Patty and Jake, b 1810, involved in Rebecca Riots 1843.

Hubert Nicholas, son to Patty and Jake, b 1813, also involved in Rebecca Riots 1843.

Jemima Nicholas, cobbler woman from Fishguard 1797. Featured in French Invasion story.

Brendan O'Connell, Michael's son, b 1801. Saved by Joseph Harries 1806. Wife Mary and 6 children. Fled from the Potato Famine 1848. Settles at Garfeth.

Michael O'Connell, leader of Irish itinerant labourers 1806.

Daniel O'Connell (false name) Irish political assassin 1806. Killed Alban Watkins 1806. Died in shipwreck 1848.

Jac Ovens (Jac Blossom) gardener at the Plas 1826-36. Died 1840.

Bowen Owen, cousin of Will 's, from Blaenffos, 1844.

John Owen, Squire of Gelli Fawr (son) b 1770, m 1802, squire from 1822,. Children Mefin. b 1804, Sara. b 1805, Gwen, b 1808, Alban, b 1810, d 1830. Enemy of Martha. Villain in Rebecca Riots, executed 1845.

Philip Owen (father), Gelli Fawr, bad squire, b 1740, d 1822. In third book, 1808.

Mefin Owen, b 1804 (son of John Owen). Married 1826. Took over as squire 1845 (on a diminished estate). Magistrate -- enemy of Martha in last story. Murdered 1855.

Frederick Owen, b 1829, d 1839, aged 10. Son of Mefin.

William Parlby, Major in 4th Light Dragoons, 1845 in Rebecca Riots.

Walter Phillips, Ambleston, b 1770, m Ellie 1808. Three children, enemy of Martha. Died 1845.

Jeb Phipps, tenant at Brithdir after purchase in 1804. Died 1826.

William Potts, Parrog, temporary and reluctant constable 1806.

Martin Price Very Nice -- tailor from Newport 1796-1830.

Character List

Owen Pritchard, b 1780, wife Sally, tenants at Dolrannog Uchaf 1806.

Nathan Probert, corn merchant, Fishguard in 1797. Died 1819.

William Probert (Will Final Testament). Lawyer from Newport,
     b 1755, d 1833.

Ellis Prosser, Frongoch, old squire, friend of Grandpa. Died 1810.

Lisbeth Prosser, Frongoch, tutor for the children 1811-1815, m 1815.

Stephen Prosser, Frongoch, younger brother of squire, d 1845,
     aged 95. Ally of Martha. Friend of Elijah Collins.

Edward Rees, Mayor of Newport 1839.

Thomas Rees (Twm Carnabwth) lived near Glynsaithmaen, cousin of
     Will. Leader of the first Rebecca Riot.

Abraham Rhys y Felin, miller from Cilgwyn Mill.

Brynmor Rhys, landlord, Black Lion inn in 1797.

Ioan Rhys of Cenarth, young squire. Married Betsi 1818. Eventually
     settled at Brithdir Mawr.

Benjamin Rice, Squire of Pentre Ifan, b 1740, m Maria 1770 (d 1802),
     transported 1798. Died on the way to Australia. Villain in the
     first story.

Joseph Rice, b 1776, only son of Benjamin Rice, Squire of Pentre Ifan,
     who was transported to New South Wales 1798. Mother Maria
     died in a lunatic asylum 1802. Killed in prison Dec 1806. Per
     secutor of Patty Ellis.

Richard John Rice, distant cousin of Joseph Rice, b 1799,
     Lieutenant in Light Dragoons 1843, enemy of Martha, Colonel
     in Dragoons 1855. Murdered 1854.

Shoni Richard (Shoni Transportation) carter and merchant from
     Newport, d 1836.

Tom Richard (Tom Transportation), waggoner in 1845, son of Shoni.

Barti Richards, one of the Stag and Pheasant Gang -- killed by
     Martha in 1844.

Mary Roberts, obsessed with Amos, and spied on Amos and Martha
     in the wood in 1846. Suicide 1846.

John Salmon, cottager at Brithdir Bach. In third story.

George Shinkins, local thug in Newport.

Samson Shinkins, merchant / shipowner / importer from Parrog.

Character List

Dafydd Shinkins, son, merchant in 1845.

Julius Smyllie of London, worked as a corrupt clerk in the Chancery Court until jailed. Released 1805 after 8 years hard labour. Transported 1807. Villain involved in treasure hunt.

Mary Jane Stokes, born 1775. Daughter of Squire John Laugharne of Pontfaen, and Owain's sister. Martha's best friend. Married Dafydd Stokes of Trecwn in 1800. Son William, b 1804, son Samuel, b 1811

Samuel Stokes, b 1811, heavily involved in Rebecca Riots. Friend of Martha 1847.

Daniel Thomas, new Mayor of Newport (also Coroner) in 1806.

Llewelyn Thomas, rector of Newport 1824-1875. Enemy of Martha.

John Thomas, senior deacon of Capel Brynberian in 1846.

Ceredig ap Tomos, Squire of New Moat, in love with Martha for years. Born 1769. Committed suicide after cancelled wedding, 24 Aug 1822. In third story.

Solomon Tomos, Fachongle Isaf (strict Caersalem) good but very intolerant.

Zeke Tomos Pencrugiau, b 1800, tenant on Bayvil estate 1837. One of *Ceffyl Pren* gang. Killed by Martha 1844. Villain during Rebecca Riots.

Charlie Toms, Churchwarden and one of the Overseers of the Poor 1800-08. Involved the adoption of Brynach.

Bobby Toms, Clerk to the Justices in 1846.

Billy Truscott, smuggler west of Fishguard 1800.

Moll Truscott (Moll Liberal Favours) prostitute from Fishguard, sister of Billy.

Thomas Tucker (b 1760, d 1825), wife Mary and three children, tenants at Penrhiw to 1825.

Waldo Tucker, oldest son, b 1790, took over as Penrhiw tenant 1825. Died Dec 1844. No heirs.

Tomos Turner, wood turner from Newport 1800.

Jonas Vaughan, Castlebythe, elderly squire, feeble but honest.

Aaron Voyle, b 1780, tenant at Llystyn after purchase 1817. Involved in Rebecca Riots.

Character List

Shoni Wallis (Shoni Hallelujah), deacon of Bethesda 1797.

Benji Walter, corn merchant from Parrog. Married Bessie, died 1802 in accident

Alban Watkins, b 1755, Squire of Llannerch, transported to NSW in 1799. Murdered in 1806. Wife Myfanwy and daughters Rose and Daisy moved to Scotland after loss of the estate in 1797. Villain in first and second books.

Benjamin Watkins, old cousin of Alban, merchant in Newport 1806.

Thomas Watkins, b 1795, nephew of Alban Watkins, Mayor in 1853. Squire of Ffynnonddofn. Enemy of Martha in last book. Executed 1855.

Billy Webb, constable in 1846.

Elijah Willaby, corrupt clerk at the Court of Chancery 1797. Then convicted, died on prison ship 1798.

Alexander Williams, Langton, b 1794, tutor for the children 1815-1818, took over Langton estate 1820.

Caradoc Williams (b 1761, d 1818) and wife Bethan. Tenant farmer at Gelli; also manager of the Sea Quarry at Aber rhigian. Five children. Sian, who was nursemaid in 1800, was the oldest, b 1779.

Gwyn Williams, b 1782, son of Caradoc and Bethan, took over tenancy of Gelli in 1818. Sian's brother.

Edward Williams Langton, wealthy squire. Loan repaid 1797.

Hugh Williams, b 1796. Solicitor from Carmarthen. Heavily involved in Rebecca Riots. Wife was 25 years older -- rather a Don Juan character.

Joseph Williams, corn merchant, Fishguard.

John Wilkins Legal, young lawyer from Newport 1843.

Ethan Wilmot, tenant of Squire Fenton, farming at Pentre Ifan 1806.

Jeb Wilson, corn merchant, Parrog.

John Wilson, cooper, from Newport, involved in the scourging of Martha in 1797, most experienced constable. He helps Martha while on his death-bed 1844.

Samson Wilson, son, also a constable 1843-44. Murdered by John Owen 1844. Villain in Rebecca Riots.

12. All Diary Entries

It may well be that readers of the Saga may wish to return to favourite parts of their favourite books for a variety of reasons. I know that some readers use segments for educational purposes or even for historical research. That's fine by me -- so long as nothing is taken as accurate history! Below I have reproduced all of the diary entries in the Greencroft Books editions of the five novels. I have entered page numbers for each chapter. Please note that in the Corgi editions there may be slight differences, and of course the page numbers will not tally at all.

ON ANGEL MOUNTAIN

Martha's Story
23 August 1796 - 28 August 1797

3. Going and Coming   pp 23-35

23 August 1796 Suicide note
24 Aug Visit to Dr Harries
28 Aug Settling in at the Plas
4 Sept Introduction to staff

4. Incidents   pp 36-55

6 September 1796 About Moses
8 Sept Description of fire
12 Sept Moses as Steward?
18 Sept Moses and the stone wall
19 Sept Martha talks to Billy

20 Sept Description of wedding
22 Sept Grandpa's lucky escape
24 Sept Discovery of the cave

Gap of 2 months -- miscarriage and depression

5. Acceptance   pp 56-63

25 November 1796 Description of miscarriage etc
30 Nov 1796 Healing from Dr Harries
2 Dec Visit to Dr Harries

6. Learning   pp 64-76

5 December 1796 Advice from Bessie
7 Dec Early morning discussion with David
10 Dec The tenants
14 Dec Peasants and poverty
18 Dec Moses's plans are thwarted

7. Festivities   pp 77-103

28 December 1796 Christmas Eve at the Plas
29 Dec Christmas Day description
30 Dec Moses is rescued
2 January 1797 Calennig, New Year etc
8 Jan The Wren House. Social visits
10 Jan Up to the cave
15 Jan Hen Galan at Pontfaen

8. A Sowing of Seed   pp 104-114

17 January 1797 Moses provokes a scene. State of the poor
27 Jan Martha asks for more education
3 Feb Circulating School comes to the Plas

10 Feb Exchange of letters
12 Feb Pancakes and *Cnapan* game
20 Feb Moses and the chickens

9. Invasion pp 115-139

22 February 1797 The French Invasion
23 Feb Martha goes to Fishguard to find out more
24 Feb David's adventure described
28 Feb Moses gets the *Ceffyl Pren* treatment

10. Daffodil Time pp 140-162

3 March 1797 Ghostly tale
4 Mar Lessons start
5 Mar Visit from 3 squires
7 Mar   Moses steals barley and flees
11 Mar Barley crop sold

11. Growth pp 163-183

12 March 1797 Martha's dream
13 Mar Witness statements
14 Mar Soap making
16 Mar Spring flowers
25 Mar Flood in Cilgwyn
28 Mar Miller in trouble
31 Mar Martha accused of witchcraft
7 April Anniversary of fire
21 April On the mountain
26 April Nightmare

12. Speculations pp 184-205

5 May 1797 Talk with the wizard

10 May Rumours of sightings
13 May Martha's Birthday party
25 May Intruder at the Plas
26 May Martha becomes convinced of Moses's guilt

13. Summer Days   pp 206-224

3 June 1797 Musical evening
11 June About David's 20th birthday
18 June Dispute with squires. True Briton Society
29 June Petty Sessions at the Plas

14. Revelations   pp 225-259

3 July 1797 Lessons on finance and hay
7 July Petty Sessions at Pentre Ifan
10 July Epidemic strikes. Visit to Joseph
11 July Panic and exhaustion
12 July Joseph's miracle cure for the sickness
13 July Back to normal
15 July The sailor's tale. Martha meets Eli Davids
17 July Martha realizes how evil Moses is
20 July Brother Morys is married
26 July Conclusions about the Plas fire
30 July Social visit to Pentre Ifan

15. Descent into Hell   pp 260-308

1 August 1797 Salaries raised; Martha is pregnant
3 August Premonition of trouble ahead
5 August David and Isaac rush to London
8 August Martha in gaol
9 August Petty sessions and whipping through the street
10 August Joseph visits gaol
13 August Despair in gaol

HOUSE OF ANGELS

27 Feb Anger and confusion
28 Feb Visit from Joseph
2 March Description of St David's Day
10 March Description of funeral on 16 Feb
19 March Threshing

Ch 4. Sunshine and Shadow pp 68-100

26 March 1805 New baby arrives and Owain visits
10 April Easter. Martha goes up the mountain again
12 April Sowing barley
24 April A visit to the relatives
26 April Reading the will
27 April Disquiet about David's death
30 April Joseph's investigations

Ch 5. Summer at Last pp 101-124

29 May 1805 Depression and recovery
2 June Decision to get lessons
6 June Shearing, Tutors
8 June Decisions re haymaking etc
10 June David's birthday
13 June Decision to take control
15 June Lessons on farm economy and botany
18 June Old Squire Lloyd dies

Ch 6. High Summer pp 125-164

25 June 1805 Hay harvest and Midsummer
5 July Ffair Gurig. Dewi etc
6 Aug Return to the cave
15 Aug Duel of Rice and Lloyd
28 Aug Corn harvest and talk with Gethin Griffiths
31 Aug Talk with Patty Ellis

2 Sept Richard Fenton and visit to the *cromlech* at Pentre Ifan
8 Sept More talk with Patty
13 Sept Contemplation on the motive for David's murder

Ch 7. The Turning of the Year   pp 165-190

5 March 1806 Report on festive season. Visit from the *Mari Lwyd*
8 March Visit to Berry Sands and churchyard
25 March A strange wonder on the beach
30 March Joseph writes to the villains
9 April Martha rescues Will Owen from the Excise officers
15 April Villains in a panic -- messages from spies
23 April Visits from suitors

Ch 8. Unsettled Weather   pp 191-240

3 May 1806 Times are hard. Resentment from other squires
7 July Premonition about Alban Watkins
10 July Talk with Bessie
15 July Visit to Mary Jane
17 July Alban Watkins arrives back from the colonies
15 August Martha speculates on what others know of the treasure
16 Aug Daisy disappears and is found
17 Aug Martha watches Owain at Pandy pools
19 August Joseph visits and operates on Brendan O'Connell
21 Aug Letter from John Fenton; 10th wedding anniversary
22 Aug Background to O'Connells
24 Aug Martha talks to Joseph about the treasure etc

Ch 9. Gentle Breezes .pp 241-262

27 August 1806 News of Rice etc from Patty and Will
31 August Beating of the Bounds -- Martha finds love again
2 Sept *Ceffyl Pren* for Matthew Lloyd and Joseph Rice
10 Sept Talk with family about Owain -- they approve

DARK ANGEL

Martha's Story
15 January 1807 - 4 September 1822

PART ONE: 1807-1808

19 Jan Visitors -- Squire Fenton and wife, Joseph and Owain

25 Jan Drawing up of wedding settlement

26 Jan Talk to the Rector about Patty and Jake wedding

2 Feb Up on the mountain

3 Feb Executions in Haverfordwest -- Martha is distressed

4 Feb Dewi's birthday and chat with Joseph

5 Feb Note to Owain and reply. Matthew Lloyd's body is returned

7 Feb First sighting of the Nightwalker

Ch 3. Shades of Grey pp 75-125

10 February 1807 Five others see the Nightwalker

12 Feb Note from Owain. Anniversary of David's death

22 Feb Owain has called twice. Cnapan game and pancakes

27 Feb Reading of banns for Patty and Jake

1 March St David's Day food riot

6 March Nightwalker and strange omens. Hurricane strikes

8 March 1807 Shipwreck. Skiff and Will in trouble

11 March Bidding for Patty and Jake's wedding

12 March 1807 Excise men hunt for the silver

13 March Martha visited by Squire Price and the Excise Men

17 March Barley threshing. Owain visits again

19 March Sara's birthday. Joseph and Owain visit

20 March Letter from Elen

22 March Betsi's birthday. Discussion with Catrin about the letter

24 March Up onto the mountain

25 March Church wedding for Patty and Jake

Ch 4. Between the Lines pp 126-152

30 March 1807 Trouble over tithes. Discoveries about Price family

31 March Altercation with Grandma Jane

1 April Talk with Bessie

2 April Walk to Llannerch with the children. Invitation to Price

4 April Discussion about Elen in Haverfordwest

10 April Prices come to tea
16 April Owain calls. Nightwalker seen again, near Llannerch

Ch 5. Giving and Taking   pp 153-213

26 April 1807 Baby found on the doorstep
27 April Wet nurse found. Talk with Grandpa
28 April Talk with Bessie
29 April Martha goes to talk to Owain. Meets Nightwalker again
2 May Grandpa talks to Owain and Martha
3 May Martha is desolate. Is Kate O'Connel the mother of Brynach?
4 May   Picnic with Owain. Martha gets ready
5 May Description of the picnic. Martha's "testament to beauty"
6 May Richard Fenton, Joseph and Skiff call in
7 May Martha confronts Patty about the baby
8 May Request to Joseph to stop searching for Brynach's mother
9 May Martha decides to tell friends about the Nightwalker
10 May Owain disappears without trace

Ch 6. Dancing to the Devil's Tune   pp 214-267

15 May 1807 Search for Owain
25 May Joseph reconstructs events
27 May Talk about disappearance; Joseph almost drowns
28 May Baptism of little Brynach
30 May Martha is told off by the servants for insensitivity
31 May Message in bottle from Owain
1 June Picnic with the children. Kite flying
2 June Parents come with news of Elen
4 June Shemi and Sian in love
15 June Nightwalker seen by others -- news is around town
28 June Talk to Joseph about Nightwalker
1 July Patty seen with the Nightwalker on Parrog
2 July. Joseph confronts the mob
5 July Exorcism by Rev Devonald

Diary Entries

Ch 7 Hunting for the Devil   pp 268-287

1 August 1807 Nightwalker at Cwmgloyn
3 Aug Martha goes to Cwmgloyn
15 Aug Mob burns down Cwmgloyn cottage
25 Sept Sian and Shemi romance; rumour of Devil at Werndew
26 Sept Visit to Joseph -- tense encounter. Martha is furious
27 Sept Bessie sorts Martha out -- apology to Joseph

Ch 8 For Better, For Worse   pp 288-312

7 April 1808 Brynach's first birthday
10 April Review of plans for servants etc
11 April Visit to the cave
25 April *Twmpath* at the Plas
30 April Ellie is married -- matchmaking for Martha
25 June Circulating School visits the Plas
12 July Nightwalker seen at Llanychaer. Squire organizes a hunt
12 July Nightwalker escapes -- Martha feels sorry for him

PART TWO: 1817-1818

Ch 9 A Matter of Trust   pp 313-336

6 April 1817 Premonition that Nightwalker will return
7 April Picnic at Carn Edward. Sighting of Nightwalker
20 April Mistress Susan Price dies. Funeral -- Nightwalker is there
23 April Review of events since 1808
27 April Martha accuses Bessie of dealings with the Nightwalker
28 April Martha has to apologize
20 May Fanny has committed suicide

Ch 10 Good Times, Bad Times   pp 337-354

21 June 1817 News of the children. To the cave in the rain
26 July 1817 Loss of hay harvest. Visit from Squire Price

226

1 Sept. Corn harvest lost. Bessie, Patty and Squire Price conspiring?

1 Dec Great hardship - estate is almost bankrupt

21 Dec Father George dies and Martha inherits £5,000

12 July 1818 Row with Daisy -- Betsi to get married

PART THREE: 1822

Ch 11 Destiny and Duty   pp 355-375

6 April 1822 Worries about Brynach's birthday

7 April 1822 Picnic at Carn Edward -- Nightwalker does not appear

8 April Billy, Shemi and Will part of the conspiracy?

14 April Joseph calls. Martha describes the death of Dewi

15 April Other disasters of 1820

10 May 1822 Martha is tired -- guilt about Daisy and Dewi

12 May Martha's 43rd Birthday. Hen party. Letter from Ceredig

25 May. Ceredig proposes and Martha accepts at last

3 July 1822. Arrangements for the wedding are complete

Ch 12 Full Circle   pp 376-412

5 August 1822 Wedding preparations. Nightwalker seen again?

21 Aug Pre-wedding reception. Owain returns -- high drama

22 Aug Owain's story is related

23 Aug Owain is ill. Martha writes to Ceredig

24 Aug Owain and Martha have a picnic and make love

25 Aug Ceredig is dead -- committed suicide

26 Aug Martha rages against social aspirations

Ch 13. In Spite of Appearances   pp 413-431

29 August 1822 Martha finally meets the Nightwalker in the cave

30 Aug Night in the cave with Iestyn..The Nightwalker's story

1 Sept Gleaning. Martha will stop writing

4 Sept Iestyn is dead. Martha grieves for him

REBECCA AND THE ANGELS

Martha's Story
1 December 1832 - 10 August 1844

PART ONE, 1832-33

Ch 2. The Cold and the Dark   pp 25-54

Ch 3. Outside, Looking in   pp 55-87

PART TWO, 1837-1839

Ch 4. Awakening   pp 88-124

16 June Green man comes. Shemi trains as a wizard (1833-36)
17 June Shemi inherits Joseph's things
25 June Harvest is in. Workhouses etc
26 June Chat with young people abt Chartists etc
15 July Still raining. Emigration etc
22 July Tithes etc. Rector's ricks are burnt
25 July Report in the *Cambrian*
3 Aug Death of Anne and her baby (2 Aug 1837)
8 Aug Funeral. Talk with Shemi
20 Aug Tithe distraint order. Martha's old chest goes
25 Aug Martha realizes Brynach is involved in riots

Ch 5. A Growing Fury pp 125-167

5 October 1837 Concern about the Turnpike Trusts
21 Oct Martha talks to Brynach; he agrees to stay out of the riots
3 March Much hardship -- *Ceffyl Pren* gang bring back the chest
15 April Up on the mountain -- visit from Squire Jobbins
22 July Hay harvest is lost. Corn warehouses are burnt
30 July Gang gets vicious -- Will and others want Martha's help
4 Aug Visit from 3 squires, who also appeal for Martha's help
5 Aug Visit from the 2 leaders of the *Ceffyl Pren* gang.
6 Dec Things get quieter. Meeting in Brynberian

Ch 6. Set upon a Certain Course pp 168-202

6th January 1839. Winter. Rescue at Carn Edward.
18th Jan News of Carmarthen events and Narberth Workhouse
19 Jan Dai and Bessie. Narberth Workhouse fire.
26th Jan Meeting of the Whitland Trust. Bullin gets the toll contract
17 March Chartist Meeting. Martha meets Hugh Williams.
25 March Talk to Havard Medical. Letter to Hugh Williams.
10 May Insurrection at Llanidloes.

Ch 7. Collision   pp 203-231

11 May 1839 Meeting at Glynsaithmaen
13 May Pwnc at Mynachlogddu. Will and Gomer off to Efailwen
14 May The first Rebecca Riot -- destruction of the Efailwen gate.
23 May The Efailwen gate is rebuilt. Gwenno and Gomer in love.
25 May Gomer and Gwenno,. Contacts with Hugh Williams.
24 June Bryn in latest riot. The dea of Rebecca is born.
28th June Riot leaders accept Rebecca idea.
19th July Third Efailwen riot. Trouble at Tavernspite.
25th July Meeting of Whitland Trust. Victory for Rebecca?

PART THREE, 1842-1845

Ch 8. A Spark in Dry Bracken   pp 232-254

3 July 1842 Letter from Hugh Williams -- Home Office wants trouble
15 July 1842 Spies are at work. Martha speculates on Govt attitudes
20 July 1842 Meeting with rioters -- Ioan convinces the men
20 Sept 1842 Good harvest. Gwenno and Gomer married.
20 Nov 1842 St Clears gates go down. Rebecca's charade.
15 Dec 1842 St Clears gates go down again.

Ch 9. A Spreading Wildfire   pp 255-274

16 January 1843. Christmas and New Year. New gates go up.
20 Jan Martha thinkst the squires have betrayed her.
24 Feb New gates are destroyed. First Rebecca Riot in Newport.
26 Feb Betrayals start -- a traitor in Newport?
27 Feb Martha lines up solicitors for future trials.
10 March Dinas gate goes down, Zeke and others arrested.
11 March Meetings re arrested men -- need to find the traitor.
12 March Petty Sessions -- all but Zeke are freed.
13 March Zeke is freed by Rebecca and hides in Martha's hay loft.

Ch 10. Smoke Signals   pp 275-304

3 July 1843. Martha confides in Tom Foster of the *Times*
15 July Zeke still in the loft -- Martha decides he must leave
17 July   Zeke is almost recaptured. Who is the traitor?
18 July Martha tries to find out who was behind the arrest warrant
25 July The riots spread far afield. Petty criminals involved
3rd August 12 more gates to go down. Bobby Morris is the traitor
4 August Bobby Morris is fed false information
8 August Gates go down - confusion among Trusts and magistrates

Ch 11. Too Close to the Flames   pp 305-325

14 August 1843. Owen's spies are dealt with by the *Ceffyl Pren*
16 Aug Eynon disappears. Petty Sessions. Spies are found guilty
17th Aug Walk on the mountain with grandson David
19 Aug Dragoons arrive in town
28 Aug Martha plays games with the soldiers
30 Aug Martha is ticked off by Bessie and Liza
8 Sept Martha feels detached and benevolent

Ch 12. Burnt Fingers   pp 326-342

25 September 1843 Fishguard Insurrection. Murder at Hendy
13 Nov Wholesale arrests
14 Nov More news about arrests
16 Nov Bryn is dead. Petty Sessions. All prisoners released.
20 Dec Inquest into Bryn's death. Bobby Morris is killed.

Ch 13. Inferno   pp 343-365

4th Jan 1844 Royal Commission completes its work.
5th Jan Martha tells the servants of her mad [plan.
26th Jan Planning meeting at Trecwn. Martha gets consent to attend
27th Jan Patty calls Martha to the deathbed of John Wilson

FLYING WITH ANGELS

Ch 3. Secrets and Lies   pp 77-114

21 July 1845 Talk with Rose about diaries etc
27 July About Jones Minor Prophet
22 Aug Corn harvest -- Brynach goes to Carmarthen
23 Aug Harvest home. Martha takes on Gerallt and Myfanwy
24 Aug Amos goes off preaching. Talk with Bessie about Amos
25 Aug Martha and the mirror
26th Aug   The estate has collapsed
1 Sept Brynach tells how it happened
2 Sept Terms of the sale to Wilmot Gwynne
3 Sept Up onto the mountain. About Daisy

Ch 4. Crossing the Gulf   pp 115-129

6 September 1845 letter from Elen
9 Sept Martha decides to tell Brynach everything
10 Sept Visit to Llanychaer and talk with Brynach
13 Sept Wilmot and Delilah Gwynne call at the Plas
20 Sept Martha wries to Elen but keeps her secrets

Ch 5. Troubled Waters   pp 130-153

5 October 1845 Visit from Daisy's 3 children
11 Oct They go back to London, with Daisy and Betsi
12 Oct Brynach tells Martha he will go to America
14 Oct Martha tells Bessie and Liza everything
24 Oct Daisy and Betsi return, full of high spirits
26 Oct News of the Potato Famine
1 Nov Martha tries divination
6 Nov Brynach and David leave for New York

Ch 6. Fire and Brimstone   pp 154-170

13 November 1845 Amos returns from his mission

18 Nov Liza is very ill
28 Nov Liza is dead
1 Dec Talk with Shemi about Amos
10 Dec Amos describes the Jones Heresy
15 Dec The Irish Famine gets worse
21 Dec Amos thunders from the pulpit

Ch 7. The Joys of Winter   pp 171-182

28 Dec 1845 White Christmas -- Gwenno has twins
12 Jan 1846 Letter from Brynach. Daisy in love
15 Feb Tom Foster passes through. Letters from New York
3 May Daisy and Havard Medical are married

Ch 8. Conduct Unbecoming pp 183-210

16 June 1846 Martha and Amos make love in the woods
17 June Start of the hay harvest
18 June Amos is ashamed, and sets out for Brecon
19 June Rumours spread about sex in the woods
20 June Martha confesses to Betsi, Rose and Daisy
24 June Martha escapes to Castlebythe for a few days

Ch 9. According to the Scriptures   pp 211-243

27 June 1846 Back to the Plas. Amos turns up. Letter to deacons
4 July Big meeting arranged for Brynberian -- Martha apprehensive
11 July Big Meeting. Chaos -- Amos is rescued by Shemi
13 July Recovering from the ordeal. Visit from Wilmot and Delilah
16 July Amos goes off to sell house. Shemi accused of murder
17 July Petty Sessions -- Shemi gets off and all celebrate

Ch 10. Hard Times pp 244-269

30 July 1846 Martha finds the body of Mary Roberts

31 July Inquest decides of suicide
1 Aug Amos returns and Mary is buried
8 Aug Delayed shock. Amos and cottage sale in Radnor
15 Aug News from America -- Amos gets a new cottage
20 Aug Tom Foster calls -- Irish famine gets worse
20 Dec Winter sets in early. Elijah Collins is dead.

Ch 11. Long Memories   pp 270-294

22 December 1846 Talk with Amos about Brynach and America
1 Feb Christmas and New Year. Martha and Amos will not marry
7 Feb Rose sees a battle in the sky
8 Feb Wilkins Legal calls -- was Elijah Collins murdered?
9 Feb Up to the cave. Bessie identifies Martha's enemies
12 Feb Discussion with friends -- Soc of Sea Serjeants
15 Feb Martha finds out more -- Sign of the anchor

Ch 12. Flotsam and Jetsam pp 295-329

8 November 1847 Martha depressed and ill. Visit to Ireland
10 Nov Martha starts Irish subscription.   Sends seed to Ireland
14 June Illness again. Amos is settled in his cottage
20 July Irish Rebellion. Goodwill evaporates. Talk with Amos
18 Aug O'Connell family shipwrecked on coast. Martha takes in the survivors
23 Aug More bodies washed up. Funerals etc
24 Aug   To the cave -- Connections with the O'Connells
25 Aug Martha talks to Amos and seeks advice from others

Ch 13. Old Scores, new Tunes pp 330-347

27 August 1848 Martha digs up the treasure
31 Aug She buys land at Garfeth for the O'Connells
10 Nov Garfeth cottage is built -- certain people are jealous
5 Dec SSS in retreat. Rose is in love

28 Oct 1849 Rose and Henry married. Martha chases Llewelyn

12 June 1850 Family all prospering. Martha is bored

Ch 14. Seeing through the Mist pp 348-364

3 September 1854 Catching up on 4 years. New threat from SSS

14 Sept Martha digs up info in the SSS

15 Sept More information from the Postman

18 Sept Martha invites Laugharne, Watkins, Howell and Rice to tea

Ch 15. Endgame pp 365-373

23 October 1854 Money for the Irish poor

29 Oct Rice and Howell are assassinated

17 Dec Death omens are seen by Martha and Amos

18 Jan 1855 Description of last Christmas at the Plas

Ch 16. Flying with Angels pp 374-396

12 February 1855 Amos is dead

13 Feb Description of the abduction and murder

14 Feb Amos has sacrificed himself to save Martha from the SSS

15 Feb Inquest is a travesty. Outrage in town

16 Feb *Ceffyl Pren* takes revenge. Amos is placed in his tomb

20 Feb Letter from Amos is delivered by Bessie

23 Feb Martha talks to her friends. Evidence for the trial

25 Feb The murderers are sent to the Assizes. Everything adds up

26 Feb 1855 Martha's farewell

============

Report from *The Cambrian*: a singular occurrence.......

13. A Brief Biography

I have been around for 66 years now, and seem to have crammed a fair amount of fun into my life! For those who enjoy biographies, some of what follows may be interesting........

I was born in Carmarthen (by accident -- it should have been in Haverfordwest) on 27th July 1940. My mother was from Carmarthenshire farming stock, but was born in South Africa while her family was out there seeking its fortune (unsuccessfully) in the diamond mines and on ostrich farms. My father was from Haverfordwest, and spent his whole working life - 50 years - working for Pembrokeshire County Council in the motor taxation department. My parents were strong Methodists, and my father was a powerful and eloquent local preacher.   They both had wonderful singing voices, and my mother could have had a career as an opera or oratorio soloist had she had different priorities. Virtually all of the family's social (not to mention religious) life was centred on Wesley Methodist Church, and that often involved three walks to the chapel and back on a Sunday, come rain or shine. On two or three evenings every week, one or both of my parents seemed to be out at some chapel meeting or other. I don't remember resenting that -- my two sisters and I just accepted that that was the norm.

We had a loving and happy childhood anyway, with holidays spent in leaky caravans in Broad Haven, Newgale and Saundersfoot. We had no car at the time, and transport was usually provided by our Uncle Dicky, who was blessed with both a car and a television set. We were very envious. Perhaps my own most memorable holidays were at my mother's family farm at Llandefaelog, not far from Kidwelly in Carmarthenshire. I hated having to eat pork fat, but I loved everything else about the farm, and have wonderful memories of haymaking and harvest, picnics for what seemed like hundreds of people in the harvesting fields, bareback rides on huge cart-horses, and hunting for eggs in the hedges. I can still smell the old Fordson

Major tractor which ran on TVO. I thought that the most exotic fellow on the whole farm was not my Uncle Ivor or any of my big cousins, but a farm servant called Handel, who lived in a little den in the hayloft above the cowshed and who slept on and under hessian sacks. He seemed to be dressed in hessian sacks too. He refused to live in the house. He lived with the cattle and for the cattle, and he was my hero. Looking back on it, I suppose that the cameraderie, mutual support mechanisms, good humour, hard labour and long working hours in the Carmarthenshire farming community must have made a deep impression on me, and I dare say that this affection for rural values comes out in the Saga.

I attended Prendergast Primary School, Haverfordwest, which was just a short walk from where we lived on Cherry Grove. Between 1951 and 1959 I attended Haverfordwest Grammar School, located on the site now occupied by the County Library. Again there are many happy memories. I worked moderately hard, and played harder, ending up as captain of the school rugby team and as the proud holder of the pole vault title at the Welsh Schools Athletics Championships. I was not really all that good at the pole vault, but I was quite smart, and on the day of the championships it poured with rain unceasingly. I cleared two or three modest heights while my pole (made of aluminium in those days) was still reasonably dry. My great rival was over-confident, came into the competition late, and slid down the pole three times, leaving me to celebrate his ignominy. I also obtained a Welsh athletics vest in competition against Scotland. I was inordinately proud of it, and kept in it a drawer for many years. It came to a glorious end, for one day when I came home from work I discovered that our small son Stephen, then in the crawling phase, was rushing about on the kitchen floor clothed in a bright red home-made garment, with the Welsh three-feather crest on his bum. My wife was very pleased. "I found this old vest in the drawer," she said happily. "Just think how much money I've saved!" They have no respect, these Swedes. At the Grammar School, I ended up as Head Boy, and enjoyed the rare privilege of being caned, while I was the holder of that august title, by our new and very fierce headmaster WG Thomas. (My crime? To have slipped away from our sports field in Portfield, in the company of all of the other prefects, to snatch a glimpse of the Taskers Girls Grammar School sports in another playing field on the other side of the road. A dastardly crime indeed.) Looking back, I suppose I must have demonstrated my lack of respect for authority, and an independent turn of mind, at a relatively early age!) I left school with A levels in Geography, English and History.

I won a place in Jesus College, Oxford. Off I went on my great adventure in 1959, and somehow managed to adjust to an alien

On some expedition or other -- can't remember which one.....

environment in which I seemed to be surrounded by super-intellectuals with social skills and levels of self-confidence which I could hardly credit. But I soon realized that there was more show than substance in all of that, and I contrived to have a whale of a time. I played a lot of rugby (and captained the college team), did some work, and missed a First by a whisker. I was having such fun that I stayed on to complete a doctorate (between 1962 and 1965) on the Ice Age in Pembrokeshire. I recall with pleasure three carefree years pottering about all over the north of the county, and I still have wonderful memories of days in the sun, all alone, looking at glacial deposits on clifftops in extremely remote places. Little wonder, then, that Mistress Martha should love her landscape so much!

While at Oxford, I organized two University Expeditions with my great friend David Sugden, one to Iceland in 1960 and another to East Greenland in 1962. That taught me a lot about planning, logistics, and even leadership, and started my love affair with exploration and the polar regions which has continued to this day. That also led to my research specialization on glaciers, the Ice Age, and climatic change, and to hundreds of articles and a string of books later on.

On completing our doctorates, both David and I obtained dream jobs with the British Antarctic Survey, and we spent the field season 1965-66 in Antarctica, looking at glacier oscillations and sea level changes in the South Shetland Islands. We visited many sites that had probably never been set foot on by human beings, even in the days of the old sealers. We learned a lot about self-sufficiency, self-reliance, and even survival. We camped in very wild places, had some narrow squeaks, and did a huge amount of very original work. We made many shore landings from the BAS ships, and also worked with helicopters based on the Royal Naval protection vessel HMS *Protector*. (There was political friction with Argentina and Chile in the Antarctic even then.) My lack of respect for authority (or for certain of my employers) also led to some interesting situations........ and then there was that famous April 1st stunt involving sacks of soggy kelp on the front steps of the Governor's residence in Port Stanley. But that's another story.

In 1966 I got a job as Geography Lecturer in Durham University, and there I stayed until 1977. I enjoyed the teaching and research enormously, but not the increasingly convoluted and time-consuming administration and university politics. While in Durham I made further research visits to the polar regions -- Arctic Canada, northern Scandinavia, and especially NW Iceland where I initiated a large research project with some small NATO funding that was on glaciers and climatic change -- almost two decades before such a thing entered the mainstream of scientific thinking. If I had dreamt up that project today, rather than thirty years ago, the research funding bodies would have thrown money at it.

In 1967 I made the biggest and happiest decision of my life and married Inger Svanholm, daughter of the Swedish Wagnerian tenor Set Svanholm. (It was almost an arranged marriage, and that's a funny story in itself. One day I'll tell it in print.) We are still in love after all these years. That's an important statement, since some people have wondered whether Martha Morgan is a sort of surrogate wife or mistress! Our two sons were born while we were in County Durham -- Stephen in 1968 and Martin in 1969. Stephen was at one time a heavy metal rock guitarist, and is now a classically trained singer based in Stockholm. Martin is married, living near Melbourne with his wife Alison and two sons Callum and Finley. They run a little candle business in the Dandenong Ranges. We try to visit them for Christmas, every second year, but of course miss them dreadfully in the intervals.

In County Durham we enjoyed a somewhat eccentric lifestyle on a run-down estate near Lanchester. We lived in a beautiful but run-down house about a mile from the nearest road and off the electricity grid. It was almost surrounded by woodland, and through the trees were the ruins of Greencroft Hall, the stable block, the walled garden, the carpenter's shop, the ice house and all sorts of other features that begged for exploration. We got all our electricity from a generator called "Fred Engine", but he died at last, and we depended thereafter upon a very smooth and efficient engine called "Charles Engine" who had nothing like as much character. We kept animals, grew a lot of our own vegetables, and tried to live off nature as far as possible -- university salaries never were very good! We still have blissful memories from that time -- Greencroft was a paradise for bringing up the two boys.

In 1976 I had a mid-thirties crisis, after a series of run-ins with my somewhat authoritarian Head of Department (there's that lack of respect for authority again!) and after being passed over for promotion. I was already writing a lot, and decided that writing and publishing would be more fun in the future than being a university professor, fighting for funds, and sitting in endless committees. Inger also wanted to start her own business. So we decided to leave Durham, much to the surprise of all our friends, who probably thought that I had had a nervous breakdown or some other psychological crisis. Far from it. I never felt more sane! We would move back to Pembrokeshire, and do our own thing. Inger would make candles, and I would write and publish, and we hoped that we could survive.

Why Pembrokeshire? Need you ask? This is the coast near Ceibwr

Above all else, we would be in charge of our own destinies. We found, through an extraordinary piece of serendipity, the perfect house with 5 acres of land, just beneath the slopes of Carningli and 2 miles from Newport. And we have survived. Inger's Pembrokeshire

Candle Centre has been going strong as a major tourist destination for 30 years, and Greencroft Books has maintained its massive publishing programme of one or two books a year over that time. I have never had to pulp or remainder anything, so I seem to get it just-about right in terms of titles and print-runs. We are both heavily involved in both businesses, as indicated on our folksy web site!

Since moving back to Wales I have concentrated on writing, publishing and marketing in order to make a living -- and have been happy to help with the building up of Inger's Pembrokeshire Candle Centre as a viable business and visitor attraction. I have also been busy in environmental protection and campaigning. I was on the Welsh Council of NCC for some years, and edited a little journal called *Nature In Wales*. I became very committed to the National Park's walks and talks programme, and did more than 200 guided walks for them over 20 years. For ten years Inger and I, helped by a few friends, organized the Newport Spring Festival of musical and other events. I organized an annual Cnapan contest between Newport and Nevern for several years (resurrecting the traditional game featured in the novels) until we had to stop it because it was impossible to get insurance cover. I still feel angry about that. With a small group of friends I started the West Wales Eco Centre in 1980, promoting the principles of energy conservation and renewable energy use and campaigning against nuclear power and large-scale fossil fuel use. Then, it was seen as a subversive organization, but we were nothing if not bloody-minded, and last year the charity celebrated its 25th anniversary. Today the Eco Centre is totally respectable because the rest of the world has caught up with us! We employ 18 people, which makes us one of the largest employers in the area; we occupy almost all of the premises in the local small business centre in Newport's old primary school; and we contribute almost £500,000 to the local economy each year. I was Chairman for many years, but now try to take more of a back seat as a humble Trustee.

Inger says that I am a professional campaigner rather than a serious writer! If only that were true -- professionals get paid, and I don't! But ever since coming back to Wales I have been active in

243

fairly high-profile grass-roots campaigning (with a lot of media work) leading to some notable successes. Looking back, I have helped to stop the building of a second nuclear plant at Trawsfynydd; to promote the adoption of wind turbines as part of a sensible energy policy; to promote the use of vegetable-based liquid fuels such as biodiesel; to stop a filthy fuel called Orimulsion from being burned at Pembroke Power Station; to highlight the financial millstone that nuclear power has hung around the neck of the British taxpayer; to promote the ideas of self-sufficiency and organic farming here in West Wales; and to stop two planned field trials of GM crops in North Pembrokeshire. A lot of my time still goes into the anti-GM campaign and into political lobbying. That all makes for an interesting life, and for some jolly encounters with officialdom -- and I hope that Mistress Martha would have approved of my priorities.

Working on the television series "Land of Dreams" for BBC2W

Hammering the Keys

Before becoming immersed in the life and times of Mistress Martha, I have had fun in the writing (and often the production) of books and booklets on a rather diverse range of topics. Jack of all trades, and master of none. But most of the titles have sold well, many have been reprinted. For the record, here are the most substantial titles:

Pembrokeshire, David and Charles, 1976
The Fishguard and Pembroke Area, Geographical Association, 1972
The Pembrokeshire Landscape, Five Arches Press, 1973 (with Robert Evans)
Scenery of Dyfed, Greencroft Books, 1976
The Milford Haven Oil Industry, Greencroft Books, 1975
Milford Haven Waterway, Pembs Coast National Park, 1981
The Rocks: Geology of Pembrokeshire, Abercastle Publications, 1973 and many reprints
Great Grandfather's Little World, Greencroft Books, 1977
Pembrokeshire Crafts and Cottage Craft Industries, Greencroft Books, 1981
Old Industries of Pembrokeshire, Greencroft Books, 1975
Wildlife in Dyfed (editor), West Wales Naturalists Trust, 1979
Welsh Pictures from Victorian Times, Greencroft Books, 1977 (hard back and paperback)
West Wales Climate and Weather, Greencroft Books, 1977
Scottish Pictures from Victorial Times, Greencroft Books, 1979 (hard-back and paperback)
Glaciers and Landscape, Edward Arnold, 1976-2000 (with David Sugden), hb and pb, reprinted many times over 25 years
Scandinavia: a new Geography, Longman, 1984
The Ice Age, Collins, 1977
The Winters of the World (editor), David and Charles/Wiley/Jacaranda 1979
The World of Ice, Orbis, 1979
Rural Crafts of Wales, Greencroft Books, 1976, 1977

Biography

Rural Crafts of England, Greencroft Books, 1979 (Susan Mosse)
Rural Crafts of Ireland, Greencroft Books, 1979 (John Jones)
The Face of the Earth, Orbis, 1980
Pembrokeshire, Pan, 1978
Alternative Wales, Greencroft Books (editor), 1982
The Ancient Game of Cnapan, Greencroft Books, 1984
Geology of Pembrokeshire, Pembs Coast National Park, 1977
Pembrokeshire, Greencroft Books, 1984
The Pembrokeshire Guide, Greencroft Books, many editions 1984-1990
Pembrokeshire Humour, Greencroft Books, 1994 and 1995
Presely Hills, Pembs Coast National Park, 1981
Ports and Harbours of Pembrokeshire, Abercastle Publications, 1974
The Carningli Walks (editor), Greencroft Books, 1995, 1999 (new
        edition)
Nuclear Power and Jobs, SEI, 1986
Honey Harfat, a Haverfordwest Miscellany, Greencroft Books, 1979,
        hardback and paperback
The Best Cardi Jokes, Greencroft Books, 1995 and 1997
Beneath the Mountain, Greencroft Books, 1998
Funny Business Down Below, Greencroft Books, 1997
Up Among the Mountain Men, Greencroft Books, 1997
Pembrokeshire Folk Tales, Greencroft Books, 1991
The Last Dragon, Greencroft Books, 1992
Fireside Tales from Pembrokeshire, Greencroft Books, 1993
More Pembrokeshire Folk Tales, Greencroft Books, 1996
How Glaciers Move, Norsk Bremuseum, 1996
Fjaerland, a Norwegian Fjordside Settlement, Greencroft Books, 1996
The Birth and Death of Glaciers, Norsk Bremuseum, 1996
Walking in the Presely Hills, Pembs Coast National Park, 1989
Pembrokeshire: Past and Present, Greencroft Books, 1995
Pembrokeshire Coast Path, HMSO-Aurum (National Trail Guide), 1990,
        1997, 2001, 2004
Pembrokeshire Ghost Stories, Greencroft Books, 1996
The Best Pembrokeshire Jokes, Greencroft Books, 2000
Pembrokeshire 2000, Greencroft Books, 1999

Biography

Walks in the World of Ice, Norsk Bremuseum, 1999
Pembrokeshire Wizards and Witches, Greencroft Books, 2001
On Angel Mountain (fiction), Greencroft Books, 2001
House of Angels (fiction), Greencroft Books, 2002
Dark Angel (fiction), Greencroft Books, 2003
Rebecca and the Angels (fiction), Greencroft Books, 2004
Flying with Angels (fiction), Greencroft Books, 2005

My favourite ash tree -- one of the copse of trees around Carningli Lodge. This is where the first cuckoo of spring is always heard

14. Some Sources

It would be quite impossible for any author to write a work of historical fiction (let alone a series of five books) without a great deal of reading and preparation. I have used the web a lot, especially since the acquisition of broadband; but there is no substitute for good old-fashioned books, which you can pile onto the floor beside your desk and leave open at important pages, much to the irritation of your wife. I have a very worthwhile library of my own, and have been lucky enough, during the writing process, to have been able to pop into the room next door as and when necessary in order to pluck some crucial tome from the bookcase. That is a faster process than hunting about on the web with the aid of Google.   Here is a list of some of the books on which I have come to depend:

Aitchison, J and Carter, H. *A Geography of the Welsh Language 1961 - 1991* (Cardiff 1994)

Archer, F. 1972 *Hawthorn Hedge Country*, Country Book Club, 188 pp

Austen, Jane 1813 *Pride and Prejudice*, republished in Penguin Classics 1995

Carey, p. 2000 *True History of the Kelly Gang*, Faber & Faber, 424 pp

Charles, B.G. *The Place-Names of Pembrokeshire* (Nat Library of Wales, 2 vols, 1992)

Children, G. and Nash, G. *Neolithic Sites of Cardiganshire, Carmarthenshire and Pembrokeshire* (Logaston Press, 1997)

Cobbett, W. 1823 *Cottage Economy*, reprinted 1974, Landsmans Bookshop, 200 pp

Collins, Wilkie, 1860 *The Woman in White*, 1994 edition, Penguin Classics, 569 pp

Cordell, A. 1976 *Hosts of Rebecca*, Coromnet, 252 pp

Davies, J.C. 1911 *Folk-lore of Mid and West Wales*, Welsh Gazette, Aberystwyth, 341 pp. (reprinted by Llanerch Publishers 1992)

Davies, R. 2005 *Hope and Heartbreak*, Univ of Wales Press, 559 pp

Donaldson, W. 2002 *Brewer's Rogues, Villains and Eccentrics*, Cassell, 662 pp

Drury, E. 1981 *Victorian Household Hints*, Aura, 160 pp

Etheridge K. 1997 *Welsh Costume in the 18th and 19th Century*, Christopher Davies, 112 pp

Evans, E. 1986 *Revival comes to Wales*, Evangelical Press of Wales, 131 pp

Evans, I (ed) 1991 *Brewer's Dictionary of Phrase and Fable*, Cassell, 1220 pp

Evans Wentz, W.Y. 1911 *The Fairy -Faith of the Celtic Countries* (Re print 1981), Humanities Press, Bucks, 524 pp.

Fenton,R. 1811 *A Historical Tour through Pembrokeshire*, London, 388pp. (reprinted by Dyfed CC 1994)

Fowler, B. 1990 *The French Invasion at Fishguard*, Dyfed CC, 34 pp

Gibbon, G. 1932 *A Scots Quair*, republished 1995, Canongate, 221 pp

Howells, W. 1831 *Cambrian Superstitions*, Longman, London,

194 pp. (reprinted by Llanerch Publishers 1991)

Howells, B. (ed) 1987   *Pembrokeshire* County History, Vol 3 , Haverfordwest

Howell, D.W. 2000 *The Rural Poor in Eighteenth-century Wales*, University of Wales Press, 317 pp

Hughes, Anne 1992   *The Diary of a Farmer's Wife 1796-1797*, Penguin, 152 pp

Hughes, K. 1998 *Everyday Life in Regency and Victorian England* (Writer's Guide), Writer's Digest, 248 pp

Hughes, R. 1996 *The Fatal Shore*, Harvill Press, 688 pp

Jones, E. 1978 *Folk Tales of Wales*, Gomer, Llandysul, 135 pp.

Jones, F. 1996 *Historic Houses of Pembrokeshire*, Brawdy Books

Jones, F. 1998 *Treasury of Historic Pembrokeshire* , Brawdy Books

Jones, J.V. 1999 *The Last Rising*, Univ of Wales Press, 273 pp.

Jones, T.G. 1930 *Welsh Folk-Lore and Folk Custom* (Reprint 1979), Brewer, Cambridge, 255 pp.

Sources

Laws, E. 1888 *The History of Little England Beyond Wales*, Bell, London, 458 pp. (reprinted by Dyfed CC 1995)

Le Faye, D. 2002 *Jane Austen -- the World of her Novels*, Frances Lincoln, 320 pp

Lewis, M. 1996 *Newport Pem and Fishguard* , Archive Photographs Series, Chalford Publishing, 128 pp.

Miles, D. *History of Haverfordwest*, Gomer, 1999

Miles, D. 1998 *A Book on Nevern*, Gwasg Gomer, 115 pp.

Miles, D. 1967 *Newport in Pembrokeshire* -- official guide, Newport, 62 pp.

Miles, D. 1996 *The Ancient Borough of Newport in Pembrokeshire*, Dyfed CC, 144 pp.

Molitorisz, S. 1998 *Australian Bush Rangers*, Murray David, 62 pp

Molloy, P. 1983 *And they blessed Rebecca*, Gomer, Llandysul

Morris, M.1899 *The Folklore of South Pembrokeshire*, microfiche held in Pembrokeshire County Library. (ms No 4.308, Cardiff Central Library)

Morris, R.M. 1989 *The Rebecca Riots* (GCSE Case History), OUP, 51 pp

Owen, Bryn 1995 *History of the Welsh Militia and Volunteer Corps 1757 - 1908,* Bridge books, 136 pp

Owen, George 1603 *The Description of Pembrokeshire* (ed. by Dillwyn Miles, reprinted 1994), Gomer, 319 pp

Owen, Trevor M. 1968 *Welsh Folk Customs*, Welsh Folk Museum, 189 pp.

Pascoe, P. *Pride and Prejudice* (York Notes), Longman, 96 pp

Pool, D. *What Jane Austen ate and Charles Dickens knew*, Robinson, London, 396 pp

Pugh, J. 1987 *Welsh Witches and Warlocks*, Gwasg Carreg Gwalch, Llanrwst, 120 pp.

Rees, S. *Dyfed: Cadw Guide to Ancient and Historic Wales* (Cadw/ HMSO, 1992)

Rees, V. 1976 *South -West Wales*, Shell Guide

Rhys, J. 1901 *Celtic Folklore : Welsh and Manx* (2 Vols), Oxford, 717pp.

Sharkey, J. 1994 *Pilgrim Ways, Ancient Landscapes*

Sikes, W. 1880 *British Goblins* (Reprint 1973), E.P. Publishing, Wakefield, 412 pp. (reprinted by Llanerch Publishers 1991)

Smith, E. 1986 *Crime and Punishment in England and Wales*, Gomer, 56 pp

Smith, G. 1989 *Smuggling in the Bristol Channel 1700 - 1850*, Countryside Books 176 pp

Smith, P. *Houses of the Welsh Countryside* (Royal Commission on Ancient Monuments, 1988)

Speake, J. 2000 *Oxford Dictionary of Idioms*, OUP, 395 pp

Speed, P.F. 1976 *The Potato Famine and the Irish Emigrants* (Then and There Series) Longman, 96 pp

Stevens, C. 1993 *Welsh Courting Customs*, Gomer, 198 pp

Toibin, C. and Ferriter, D. 2002 *The Irish Famine*, Profile Books, 214 pp

Trevelyan, M. 1909 *Folk-Lore and Folk-Stories of Wales*, Stock, London, 350 pp

Trollope, G. 2003 *The Cambrian 1804-1930*, T Publishers, 176 pp

Vaughan, H.M. 1926 *The South Wales Squires*, Methuen, London, 216 pp.

Vince, J. 1985 *Power Before Steam*, John Murray, 160 pp

Wallace-Hadrill, F.G. 1989 *The Parish Church of St Mary, Newport, Pembs*, Newport, 28 pp

Whitlock, R. 1965 *A Short History of Farming*, John Baker, 246 pp

Williams, D. 1955 *The Rebecca Riots*, Univ. of Wales Press, Cardiff, 377 pp.

Wilson, C. 1991 *The Giant Book of the Supernatural*, Paragon, 567 pp